THE NEW CAMBRIDGE HISTORY
OF INDIA

Vijayanagara

THE NEW CAMBRIDGE HISTORY OF INDIA

General editor GORDON JOHNSON
Director, Centre of South Asian Studies, University of
Cambridge, and Fellow of Selwyn College

Associate editors C. A. BAYLY
Smuts Reader in Commonwealth Studies, University of
Cambridge, and Fellow of St Catharine's College

and JOHN F. RICHARDS
Professor of History, Duke University

Although the original Cambridge History of India, published between 1922 and 1937, did much to formulate a chronology for Indian history and describe the administrative structures of government in India, it has inevitably been overtaken by the mass of new research published over the last fifty years.

Designed to take full account of recent scholarship and changing conceptions of South Asia's historical development, The New Cambridge History of India will be published as a series of short, self-contained volumes, each dealing with a separate theme and written by a single person. Within an overall four-part structure, thirty-one complementary volumes in uniform format will be published during the next five years. As before, each will conclude with a substantial bibliographical essay designed to lead non-specialists further into the literature.

The four parts planned are as follows:

I The Mughals and their Contemporaries.

II Indian States and the Transition to Colonialism.

III The Indian Empire and the Beginnings of Modern Society.

IV The Evolution of Contemporary South Asia.

A list of individual titles in preparation will be found at the end of the volume.

THE NEW
CAMBRIDGE
HISTORY OF
INDIA

I · 2

Vijayanagara

BURTON STEIN

The right of the
University of Cambridge
to print and sell
all manner of books
was granted by
Henry VIII in 1534.
The University has printed
and published continuously
since 1584.

CAMBRIDGE UNIVERSITY PRESS

CAMBRIDGE

NEW YORK   PORT CHESTER

MELBOURNE   SYDNEY

PUBLISHED BY THE PRESS SYNDICATE OF THE UNIVERSITY OF CAMBRIDGE
The Pitt Building, Trumpington Street, Cambridge, United Kingdom

CAMBRIDGE UNIVERSITY PRESS
The Edinburgh Building, Cambridge CB2 2RU, UK
40 West 20th Street, New York NY 10011–4211, USA
477 Williamstown Road, Port Melbourne, VIC 3207, Australia
Ruiz de Alarcón 13, 28014 Madrid, Spain
Dock House, The Waterfront, Cape Town 8001, South Africa

http://www.cambridge.org

First published 1989
First paperback edition 2005

A catalogue record for this book is available from the British Library

Library of Congress cataloguing in publication data

The new Cambridge history of India/
general editor Gordon Johnson.
associate editors C. A. Bayly and John F. Richards.
p.   cm.
Previous published: The Cambridge history of India
Bibliography: pt. 1, v. 2.
Includes index.
Contents: pt. 1, v. 2. Vijayanagara/Burton Stein
ISBN 0 521 26693 9 (pt. 1, v. 2) hardback
1. India – History.
I. Johnson, Gordon.   II. Bayly, C. A. (Christopher Alan)
III. Richards, J. F.   IV. Cambridge history of India.
DS436.N47   1989
954 – dc 19   89-690 CIP

ISBN 0 521 26693 9 hardback
ISBN 0 521 61925 4 paperback

Frontispiece: An image of Hanuman in front of
the gateway of the Hazara Rama temple.

To
DOROTHY

CONTENTS

ILLUSTRATIONS

PLATES
Between pages 50 and 51

MAPS

Frontispiece and plates 6–8 by courtesy of George Michell.
Plates 1–5 by courtesy of John Gollings.

GENERAL EDITOR'S PREFACE

The New Cambridge History of India covers the period from the beginning of the sixteenth century. In some respects it marks a radical change in the style of Cambridge Histories, but in others the editors feel that they are working firmly within an established academic tradition.

During the summer of 1896, F. W. Maitland and Lord Acton between them evolved the idea for a comprehensive modern history. By the end of the year the Syndics of the University Press had committed themselves to the Cambridge Modern History, and Lord Acton had been put in charge of it. It was hoped that publication would begin in 1899 and be completed by 1904, but the first volume in fact came out in 1902 and the last in 1910, with additional volumes of tables and maps in 1911 and 1912.

The History was a great success, and it was followed by a whole series of distinctive Cambridge Histories covering English Literature, the Ancient World, India, British Foreign Policy, Economic History, Medieval History, the British Empire, Africa, China and Latin America; and even now other new series are being prepared. Indeed, the various Histories have given the Press notable strength in the publication of general reference books in the arts and social sciences.

What had made the Cambridge Histories so distinctive is that they have never been simply dictionaries or encyclopedias. The Histories have, in H. A. L. Fisher's words, always been 'written by an army of specialists concentrating the latest results of special study'. Yet as Acton agreed with the Syndics in 1896, they have not been mere compilations of existing material but original works. Undoubtedly many of the Histories are uneven in quality, some have become out of date very rapidly, but their virtue has been that they have consistently done more than simply record an existing state of knowledge: they have tended to focus interest on research and they have provided a massive stimulus to further work. This has made their publication doubly worthwhile and has distinguished them intellectually from other sorts of reference book. The editors of the New Cambridge History of India have acknowledged this in their work.

The original Cambridge History of India was published betweeen 1922 and 1937. It was planned in six volumes, but of these, volume 2 dealing with the period between the first century A. D. and the Muslim invasion of India never appeared. Some of the material is still of value, but in many respects it is now out of date. The last fifty years have seen a great deal of new research on India, and a striking feature of recent work has been to cast doubt on the validity of the quite arbitrary chronological and categorical way in which history has been conventionally divided.

The editors decided that it would not be academically desirable to prepare a new History of India using the traditional format. The selective nature of research on Indian history over the past half-century would doom such a project from the start and the whole of Indian history could not be covered in an even or comprehensive manner. They concluded that the best scheme would be to have a History divided into four overlapping chronological volumes, each containing about eight short books on individual themes or subjects. Although in extent the work will therefore be equivalent to a dozen massive tomes of the traditional sort, in form the New Cambridge History of India will appear as a shelf full of separate but com-plementary parts. Accordingly, the main divisions are between I. *The Mughals and their Contemporaries*, II. *Indian States and the Transition to Colonialism*, III. *The Indian Empire and the Beginnings of Modern Society*, and IV. *The Evolution of Contemporary South Asia*.

Just as the books within these volumes are complementary so too do they intersect with each other, both thematically and chrono-logically. As the books appear they are intended to give a view of the subject as it now stands and to act as a stimulus to further research. We do not expect the New Cambridge History of India to be the last work on the subject but an essential voice in the continuing discourse about it.

PREFACE

The Vijayanagara kingdom ruled a substantial part of the southern peninsula of India for three centuries, beginning in the middle of the fourteenth, and during this epoch this Indian society was transformed from its medieval past toward its modern, colonial future. At the same time that its kings, or 'Rayas', were peninsular overlords and their capital, 'the City of Victory', or Vijayanagara, was the symbol of vast power and wealth, lordships of all sorts became more powerful than ever before. This resulted from the martialisation of its politics, and the transfiguring of older economic and social institutions by the forces of urbanisation, commercialisation and monetisation. These changes were gradual and only dimly perceived during the time of its first dynasts, who were content to be conquerors whose *digvijaya*, or righteous conquests, in Tamil country left the ancient royal houses of the Cholas and Pandyas in their sovereign places, except that they were reduced by their homage to the Karnatak kings of Vijayanagara.

At the zenith of their power and authority during the early sixteenth century, Vijayanagara kings were among the greatest historical rulers of India. They had reduced to subjugation numerous royal and chiefly lineages that they did not uproot and had humiliated the several Muslim sultanate regimes of Deccan. Yet, even then, the sovereignty of the Rayas remained what kingship had long been, that is, ritual, so that, beyond the heartland of their kingdom, where their hegemony and resource commanded were formidable, they were content with the homage and occasional tribute of distant lords. Moreover, they forbore, if they did not actually foster, the creation by their nominal agents of a whole set of compact and clonal kingdoms – denominated as 'nayaka kingdoms' – whose competition later helped to destroy the kingdom. For the series of which it is part, this volume seeks to sketch – it can do little more – the broad development of society in South India from its medieval foundation to its late, pre-colonial, incipiently modern, era. Because of the temporal scope of The New Cambridge History of India, this analysis is most schematic for the early times of the kingdom, hence several controversial, and the continually debated historiographical, issues are barely touched upon; these include the actual founding of the kingdom around 1340 and its ideological character then and later. Oriented as this book is toward later developments, with which other volumes of the series will be concerned, detailed and systematic treatment of the kingdom begins in the late fifteenth century and carries through the late sixteenth century. By that time, the kingdom was in crisis, unable to recover its early *élan* and overtaken by a whole set of new conditions. Yet, the idea and the structure of the Vijayanagara kingdom lived on in the smaller regimes spawned by the kingdom. These regimes and their little kingly rulers came to deny ever larger parts of the peninsula to the successors of its great sixteenth-century kings.

The Vijayanagara era was one in which I see a new form of polity, but one with important links to earlier polities in being segmentary in character and one in which kings continued to be essentially ritual figures rather than, like contemporaries in western Europe, autocrats ruling bureaucratised, absolutist regimes. But it is less in its political forms than in others, I believe, that the kingdom attains its primary historical importance. For this we must look elsewhere: to the massive architectural style that permeated all of the southern peninsula in the building and rebuilding of its temples and to the first, permanent, non-religious, or civil, buildings, including royal palaces; to the expansion of agrarian institutions as well as its new towns and its commerce over the whole of the peninsula; and to the proliferation of whole structures of local rights, or entailments, by all sorts of social groups who constitute the society over which the first of the colonial institutions came to be imposed, beginning in the late eighteenth century.

Inevitably, a work of this synthetic nature bears a large debt to the scholarship of others of which only some can be acknowledged in the text or the appended bibliographical note.

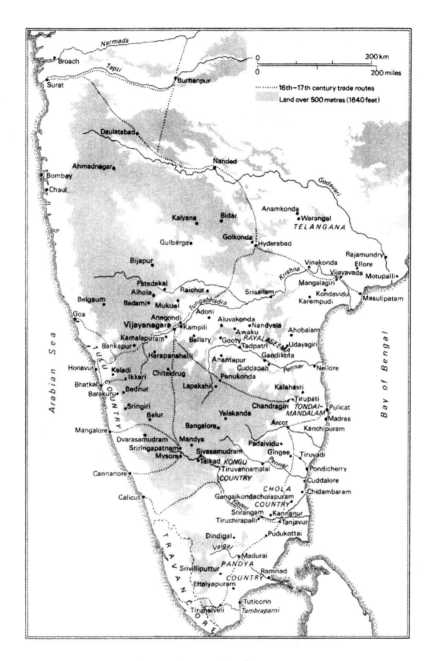

1 The southern peninsula, *c.* 1400–1500

xiii

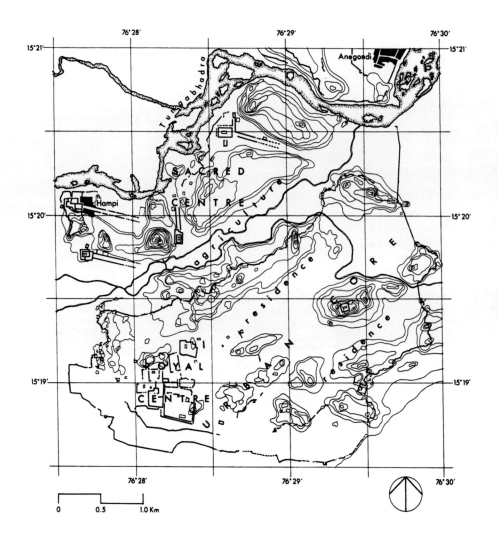

2 The city and its zones

ONE

INTRODUCTION

The kingdom or 'empire' of Vijayanagara takes its name, 'City of Victory', from its capital on the Tungabhadra River, near the centre of the sub-continent. Its rulers over three centuries claimed a universal sovereignty – 'to rule the vast world under a single umbrella' – and they also, more modestly, referred to themselves as the rulers of Karnata, modern Karnataka. This seemingly humble reduction of the scope of their suzerainty from the world to a small portion of the Indian sub-continent is somewhat deceptive. Vijaya-nagara kings seemed to have had the sense that the kingdom established in the fourteenth century revived an earlier universal sovereignty in Karnataka, that of the Chalukyas of Badami (ancient Vatapi in Bijapur district of modern Karnataka). Vijayanagara kings adopted the emblem of the Chalukyas, the boar, or *varaha*, and perhaps quite consciously modelled their capital on the Chalu-kyan capitals of Vatapi and Aihole of the sixth to eighth centuries, though Vijayanagara in 1500 was a great fortified place covering 10 square miles, dwarfing the Chalukyan cities. Even so, the first temples which they built in the city were somewhat enlarged replicas of those found at Chalukyan capitals.

Also as with the Chalukyas, there were several distinct lineages, or dynasties, of Vijayanagara rulers. The first of these was some-times called Yadavas, but was more often known as Sangamas, for the chief whose sons established the kingdom around 1340. Descendants of one of the sons of Sangama, who ruled as Bukka I (reign, 1344–77), expanded the city and realm until the late fifteenth century when a second, or Saluva, ruling line was established briefly by a Vijayanagara generalissimo, Saluva Narasimha. In 1505, a third dynasty came into being called Tuluvas, suggesting that they came from the coastal part of Karnataka called Tulu. Under their four decades of rule, the realm reached its greatest extent and its rulers their greatest power. The last Vijayanagara dynasty, of the Aravidu family, assumed authority in 1542; it was named for another generalissimo, Aravidi Bukka, whose sons founded a line of rulers; members of this family held diminished imperial authority until the late seventeenth century when, as a result of repeated invasions from Muslim states to the North and civil wars within, Vijayanagara authority was fragmented among a set of smaller, independent regional domains tracing their ruling credentials from the kingdom.

Among Indian kingdoms, a rule of three centuries is very long, and this together with the large territory over which Vijayanagara kings reigned makes it one of the great states in Indian history. The realm can be defined by the provenance of royal inscriptions over some 140,000 square miles, about the same area as the Madras Presidency in 1900, when the first histories of Vijayanagara appeared.

HISTORIOGRAPHY

However, a century before, when the presidency was taking the shape that it was to have until 1947, two partial accounts of Vijayanagara were presented to the English-speaking world, the first by Mark Wilks in 1810 and the second by Colonel Colin Mackenzie in 1815. It was to be another century before Vijayanagara history was taken up again, by Robert Sewell, in 1900.

Wilks's work was prepared while he was the political agent ('resident') for the East India Company at the court of the rajas of Mysore, after the Wodeyar rajas had been reinstalled in 1799 on a throne seized some forty years before by Haidar Ali Khan. The basis of Wilks's reconstruction was an eighteenth-century Kannada language work, written on a cotton scroll, by a Brahman savant known as Pootia Pundit. Colin Mackenzie, a military surveyor turned antiquarian, collected this and other accounts as well as making copies of numerous inscriptions from all over Madras and Mysore. He was aided by a set of learned Indians who copied and translated temple inscriptions and 'traditional histories' around 1800, which became the first sources of the reconstruction of early Indian history; they also collected artifacts that became exhibits in the first museums in India.

Mackenzie only once offered an interpretation of these sources; this was in an address he delivered to the Asiatic Society of Bengal on 5 April 1815, though not published in the journal of the Society until 1844. However, the direct participation of Indians in the

Mackenzie collections makes their writings of historical accounts of Vijayanagar among the first in which Indians presented something of their own history.

Sewell, like his two English predecessors, was an official, and as a member of the Madras civil service he was charged with collecting information about the south Indian past and with publishing works on inscriptions and antiquarian remains in the Madras Presidency. This task he carried out, like Wilks and Mackenzie before him, with the help of Indians, whose knowledge of Sanskrit, Tamil, Telugu, Kannada, and Malayalam – the historical and modern languages of the southern peninsula – was essential and whose experience with Sewell prepared some of them to carry out independent researches which were published during the early years of the twentieth century. All of this continued investigations begun a century before under Mackenzie and with the same purpose.

These Britons at opposite ends of the nineteenth century sought to devise an historical past not for the sake of pure knowing, but for the purpose of controlling a subject people whose past was to be so constructed as to make British rule a necessity as well as a virtue.

This intention is exemplified in the only popular work published by Sewell in 1900, *Forgotten Empire (Vijayanagar)*. Here, an outline of the genealogical and chronological evidence on the dynasties of Vijayanagara was briefly presented, followed by two long and historically configuring translations of the accounts of two sixteenth-century Portuguese visitors to the city. These Portuguese merchant adventurers knew no Indian languages well enough to correct their visual impressions through understandings obtained from verbal or written views of Indians. Vijayanagara kings of the sixteenth century were presented as oriental despots whose authority consisted partly of sacred power founded upon, or regenerated by, royal sacrifices and partly on feudal relations between them and great territorial lords ('captains'). Finally, to these was added the orientalist notion of the fabulous riches of Asia which was supported by the splendours of the city itself, its vastness, its monumentality, and the wealth of its citizens.

Chronicles of the sixteenth-century Portuguese visitors have become important fixtures in the historiography of Vijayanagara, and rightly, because these were not mere inventions. The royal ceremonies they described have since been authenticated by enactments in numerous royal courts in South India as well as by texts pertaining to them that were being brought into European knowledge in Sewell's time. Moreover, the vivid descriptions of the city have since been verified by archaeological research that has been carried out at Hampi, the site of Vijayanagara, by contemporary scholars from India and Europe, as well as by photography of the site that goes back to 1856.

Still, the orientalising intention of men like Sewell cannot be set aside. Though much of the epigraphical and textual analyses of Sewell and other European founders of pre-modern history in South India was done by Indians such as S.M. Natesa Sastri, H. Krishna Sastri, and S. Krishnaswami Aiyangar, it was a European intentionality that prevailed. Harsh oriental despotisms and factious local magnates were seen to have led to the dominion of Muslims in the North of India and they threatened the South as well. Despite the peril to Hindu institutions posed by Muslim powers in peninsular India after the fourteenth century, Indians, in this view, could not overcome the flaws in their political institutions. This task awaited the British; what even the great Mughals failed to achieve in India, the British would to create order and progress over the entire sub-continent.

Such views were bound to change as Indians seized control of their history. The earliest and most influential successor to Sewell was S. Krishnaswami Aiyangar. After completing his post-graduate degree in 1897 and teaching in a Bangalore college for a decade, he initiated the chair in Indian History and Archaeology established at the University of Madras in 1914. He saw Sewell's last works on the inscriptions and historical chronology of South India through publication, on the Englishman's recommendation, and by the mid-1920s Krishnaswami Aiyangar had published extensively on topics in Vijayanagara history.

He departed in two important ways from the historiography inherited from Sewell and other Europeans. One was his emphasis on Hindu–Muslim conflict as being the cause and principal shaper of the Vijayanagara kingdom and the claim that resistance to Islam was the great vindication of Vijayanagara. This view is evident in his first major historical publication, *Ancient India* (1911), which was

4

based on his MA thesis of 1898; in later work, especially in his *South India and her Muhammadan Invaders* (1921), the view about Hindu–Muslim conflict is fully worked out. There he spoke of how the last ruler of the Hoysala kingdom of Karnataka, Vira Ballala III, 'made a patriotic effort to dislodge the Muhammadans from the South ... fell in the effort, and brought his dynasty to an end in carrying on this great national war of the Hindus' and of how Vijayanagara succeeded to this 'patriotic national' mission.

This early orientation to Hindu–Muslim conflict had another important manifestation. This was a perception, held by him from 1897, that the patriotic mission of Vijayanagara was passed directly to the next great defenders of Hindu dharma, the Maratha kingdom of Sivaji. An historical connection with Vijayanagara was claimed through Shahji, Shivaji's father who had served his Bijapur sultanate masters for many years in Bangalore, the heart of the waning Vijayanagara kingdom in the seventeenth century.

Vijayanagara historiography also changed because of Krishnaswami Aiyangar's insistence that literary evidence of that period should have as much standing in the interpretations of historians as epigraphy and archaeology. From the very beginning, his writing on Vijayanagara followed this methodology. Poems of praise (*kavya*) and genealogical accounts of great families (*vamsavali*) in Sanskrit and other languages marked a return to the sources that Wilks and Mackenzie considered the most important; this shifted the focus of the previous generation of historians. Sewell and others had concentrated upon the royal families of Vijayanagara in their great capital and had relied on Portuguese chronicles and Muslim accounts such as that of Muhammad Kasim Firishtah which had been translated in 1910. Krishnaswami Aiyangar turned to the study of the numerous magnates in Karnataka and elsewhere in the 'empire', but his historical reconstructions, while based on literary sources, were always attentive to evidence from inscriptions. He insisted that the latter could only provide the 'barebones' of historical study, literary sources must do the rest. This approach was passed to his own students at the University of Madras until his retirement in 1929.

By that time, and thanks to Krishnaswami Aiyangar, the field of Vijayanagara history was well established, though it was beginning to reflect new emphases and concerns of that time. Among the more important was the rise of regional nationalism in parts of the large Madras Presidency, especially among Kannada and Telugu speakers. The important works of two young historians of the 1930s manifest this: B. A. Saletore writing on Karnataka history and N. Venkataramanayya writing on Andhra. They adopted Krishnaswami Aiyangar's reliance upon literary evidence, but differed from him in that they looked at Vijayanagara history from the core of the kingdom, in the border region between Kannada-speaking Karnataka and Telugu-speaking Andhra, rather than from either Tamil country or the perspective of the peninsula as a whole.

For Saletore, the Vijayanagara kingdom of the fourteenth century was created by the release of 'the latent energy of the Hindu Dharma in southern India' by Muslim conquest and humiliation. This view had already been given prominence by Krishnaswami Aiyangar in Madras, as well as by the Reverend Henry Heras teaching in Bombay, whose student Saletore had been. But Saletore went further with this argument. He made Vijayanagara an expression of Karnataka nationalism. Thus, in the founding of the new kingdom by the five sons of the chief Sangama

> did Karnataka vindicate to the rest of the Hindu world her honour by sending forth a little band of five brothers ... Karnataka by birth and Karnataka in valour, as the champions of all that was worth preserving in Hindu religion and culture.[1]

Saletore also insisted that 'ancient constitutional usage' in Karnataka (*purvada mariyade*) was maintained by rulers of the new kingdom even to the extent that by doing so the seeds of the kingdom's destruction were sown. Here, again, Saletore was indebted to predecessors like Krishna Sastri and Krishnaswami Aiyangar who had said that the ultimate defeat of Vijayanagara resulted from the failure of its rulers to strengthen central administrative control by diminishing the ancient authority of village and locality institutions and their leaders ranging from village headmen to 'feudatory families'.

Even as Saletore was completing his University of London doctoral thesis in 1931, from which the above quotations come,

---

[1] B. A. Saletore, *Social and Political Life in the Vijayanagara Empire* (Madras: B. G. Paul, 1934), vol. 1, p. 39.

Venkataramanayya was preparing a monograph denying the Kar-nataka-centred views of Saletore and Heras.

Two of his monographs appeared in 1933 and 1935 challenging both Karnatak historians. These works presented the counter-interpretation that the Sangama brothers who founded Vijayanagara were not Kannada speakers (or Kannadigas) but were Telugus from the Andhra coast of the Bay of Bengal and that the boar emblem that was thought to connect Vijayanagara with the ancient Karnatak kingdom of the Chalukyas of nearly a thousand years before was really borrowed from the Telugu Kakatiya kingdom of the four-teenth century. He also argued that two of the foundational institutions of the Vijayanagara state were introduced by the Telugu conquerors of Karnataka on the model of the Kakatiyas; these were the distinctive form of military land tenure called the *nayankara* system and the distinctive form of paid village servants called the *ayagar* system.

By 1940, the historiography on Vijayanagara had passed through three stages. European orientalists, using earlier Indian accounts and with the help of Indian subordinates, opened the field by having identified its major literary and inscriptional sources and its broad chronology. This largely technical phase lost its orientalist colour-ing and assumed another ideological overlay during the intermediate custodianship of scholars like Krishnaswami Aiyangar and Heras who, in their somewhat different ways, imbued Vijayanagara histo-riography with an anti-Muslim and broad nationalistic bias. From them, and with their benedictions, Vijayanagara history passed into a third phase when scholars like Saletore and Venkataramanayya saw in that history a basis for the narrower nationalism or regional patriotisms of Karnataka and Andhra.

New scholars were slowly being recruited; one was T. V. Mahal-ingam. Encouraged by K. A. Nilakanta Sastri, who succeeded Krishnaswami Aiyangar in the history chair at the University of Madras, Mahalingam undertook work on administrative and economic aspects of Vijayanagara history. This followed some of the pioneering work of Krishnaswami Aiyangar on Vijayanagara, but more especially Nilakanta Sastri's own work on the Tamil Chola dynasty of the ninth to thirteenth centuries in which adminis-trative history was accorded new saliency. Mahalingam and others

added to the rich, detailed, and diverse historiography on Vijayanagara that had emerged by the 1940s; they explored the rise and fall of
numerous chiefly families everywhere, their alliances and their
oppositions to the Vijayanagara imperial order as well as the
conquests of its kings, or rayas,[2] and their occasional humiliations.
But none had yet surpassed the breadth of vision of Krishnaswami
Aiyangar during the early years of the twentieth century.

In 1919, he had inaugurated the University of Madras historical
series with the publication of *Sources of Vijayanagar History*. The
latter work consisted of one hundred texts and translations from
inscriptions and literary works, including chronicles on various
Vijayanagara kings and great families of the age. The historical series
was ably continued under Nilakanta Sastri as professor of Indian
history and archaeology from 1929 to 1947; it became the vehicle for
major publications on Vijayanagara during the 1930s and 1940s, and
all reflected the imprimatur of its distinguished editor.

The impact of Nilakanta Sastri upon Vijayanagara history was
profound, though he published no monographic research in the
field. He had taken up one of the strands of Krishnaswami
Aiyangar's wider-ranging scholarship – that on Chola administrative history – and made it the focus of his major work on the Chola
kingdom. Nilakanta Sastri's scepticism about historical sources
other than inscriptional ones made some of his writings different
from that of Krishnaswami Aiyangar and from that of some of his
own students at Madras. Venkataramanayya and Mahalingam, for
example, depended heavily on literary sources; both used the local
traditions collected by Colin Mackenzie during the early nineteenth
century where it was maintained at the Oriental Manuscripts
Library of the University of Madras; both also used poetical works
as well as Muslim and Portuguese chronicles. In that, they and their
younger colleagues seemed to be defying Nilakanta Sastri's efforts
to construct a history of pre-modern South India free from the
quirkiness of Indian literary evidence that had drawn the disdain of
European historians from Macaulay in the 1830s onward. To
Nilakanta Sastri, the way to a historiography that Europeans could
admire was through reliance upon the relatively chaste, datable, and
locatable epigraphical records, of which tens of thousands had been

---

[2] The Sanskrit 'raja' and its derivative 'raya' mean 'king'.

collected in South India, and by casting interpretations of these fragmentary data in a universal frame that showed medieval South Indian administrative institutions to be of the same quality as European ones. This ambition was partially manifested in the delineation by Venkataramanayya and Mahalingam of so-called 'central', 'provincial', and 'local government' administrative levels in Vijayanagara times, though they managed no better than their teacher to resolve contradictions posed by these variously perceived levels.

Nilakanta Sastri's major contributions to Vijayanagara history were of another sort. One was his sponsorship of a three-volume *Further Sources of Vijayanagara History* in 1946, edited jointly with Venkataramanayya; another was his long, synthetic chapters on Vijayanagara in his *A History of South India*, first published in 1955.

Further Sources followed the pattern of Krishnaswami Aiyangar's collection of sources in 1919; it was justified on the grounds that 'Hindu literary sources' corrected the bias of Muslim chronicles and 'foreign' accounts. This justified the use of the 'Mackenzie Manuscripts'. The first volume of *Further Sources* consisted of a 369-page introduction to the document by Venkataramanayya and constituted one of the few general histories of Vijayanagara since the early works of Sewell and Krishnaswami Aiyangar; the pioneering scholarship of the latter received little notice from Venkataramanayya except for minor corrections. Still, this 'introduction' harked back to Krishnaswami Aiyangar's political understandings in two ways. One was in seeing Vijayanagara history as a heroic struggle to protect dharma from Islam – 'the last glorious chapter of the independent Hindu India of the South'; the other was in seeing the polity of Vijayanagara to be about relations among great warrior families, rather than about conventional, centralized administration. In the latter view, Venkataramanayya implicitly repudiated Nilakanta Sastri's conception of the medieval south Indian state, in particular, the latter's interpretation of Chola history as having precociously anticipated the modern centralised, bureaucratic state. Such a Chola model still lurked in the characterisation of the Vijayanagara political system of Nilakanta Sastri's *History of South India*, but different conditions were seen to have made for different political arrangements. Hence, Nilakanta Sastri took Vijayanagara as a centralised, 'hereditary monarchy', which was prevented from achieving full central authority because of the constant threat from Muslim states and the 'intransigence of [its] feudatories'. Both external and internal threats to Vijayanagara produced 'the nearest approach to a war-state ever made by a Hindu kingdom'. And though central authority failed to be realised, autonomous local Tamil institutions, which Nilakanta Sastri admired, were fatally weakened, having 'suffered abridgment as their officials came to be linked more and more closely with the central government'.

Nilakanta Sastri's efforts in the 1950s to make Vijayanagara out to be a centralised empire has influenced subsequent writing on in two ways, both negative. One was in A. Krishnaswami Pillai's *The Tamil Country under Vijayanagara* (1964). The politics of the kingdom are seen by him as 'feudal' everywhere in the southern peninsula, but especially in Tamil country on which his work concentrated. His was an attempt to provide a positive foundation for the Vijayanagara state, something better than Nilakanta Sastri's, which rested weakly on a conception of flawed centralism. However, Krishnaswami Pillai's appliqué of feudalism is unpersuasive and diminishes a monograph otherwise rich in detailed analysis, whose main thrust recalls the earlier works of Krishnaswami Aiyangar and Venkataramanayya. A second negative reaction to Nilakanta Sastri's treatment of Vijayanagara came from the present author in his *Peasant State and Society in Medieval South India* of 1980. The latter work on Chola history was concerned to present an alternative to the centralised political conception of Nilakanta Sastri. Accordingly, the idea of a 'segmentary state' was proposed as appropriate for the Cholas as well as for Vijayanagara.

In broad terms, that argument of several years ago is still considered valid, and it informs the present historiographical discussion and the rest of this study of late Vijayanagara. There are differences between my 1980 formulation and the present study that should be noted here. One certainly is an acknowledgement of criticism of some aspects of the argument in the Vijayanagara sections of *Peasant State and Society in Medieval South India* prompting certain corrections. Another is the incorporation here of the work that has been achieved in several different international collaborations on Vijayanagara in recent years: the impressive joint

studies conducted by Japanese and Indian scholars on the pre-
modern economy of South India; the work that has been done by
archaeologists, architectural historians and others at Hampi, the site
of the Vijayanagara capital of old; and the recent and continuing
studies by Indian and other scholars of Telugu and Tamil literature
of the Vijayanagara era. All of these contribute to the present work
as well as leading back to the place of S. Krishnaswami Aiyangar in
the whole historiographical enterprise on Vijayanagara.

Nilakanta Sastri made the centre of his interpretive analysis the
onslaught of Islam. The military consequences of this led to what he
called the 'war state' of Vijayanagara. However, such militarisation
would surely have come with the Europeans in the sixteenth century
as indeed it did in the form of guns, mercenaries, and war horses
then. The effects, too, would have been the same in disrupting the
system of medieval political relations. Disruption of older forms
became an irreversible transformation when to the changes in the
levels of force came changes in levels of the economy, especially
commercial developments. The combined impact upon peninsular
India from two massive forces operating in Eurasia – the expanding
Islamic 'gunpowder empires' of the Middle East and Mughals of
India as well as the sixteenth-century expansion of Europe –
generated transforming forces of such military and commercial
significance as to render the old regime of medieval South India
impossible to sustain. The demand for Indian spices and textiles
inevitably grew and with that the massive import of bullion, a
conjuncture that could not but alter ancient peninsular forms.
Krishnaswami Aiyangar's openness about the evolving structure of
society and politics in the peninsula gives his work of the early
twentieth century a remarkable freshness, especially for its readiness
to be aware of some of the new forces at work. Thus, in his
treatment of the complex relations among the rulers of the Deccan
sultanates and the numerous regimes of great warrior families
throughout the South, his writings suffered less of the conventional
regrets about the fissiparous forces that weakened Vijayanagara in
its sacred, dharmic mission. He also eschewed the centrist bias of
many later Vijayanagara historians that saw Hindu opponents of a
Vijayanagara peninsular hegemony as anti-nationalist. In these, he
exhibited a greater detachment from the presentistic preoccupations

of his time than many of his contemporaries and successors. We are therefore now permitted to see in his work possibilities for understanding that were unfortunately closed off in the work of many that came after him.

TWO

THE MEDIEVAL PAST: CONTINUITY
AND DISJUNCTION

If the interpretative lead of S. Krishnaswami Aiyangar and some historians of Maharashtra is followed, then Vijayanagara was the precursor of and the precedent for the Maratha state of the seventeenth century. Yet, Vijayanagara was also a medieval south Indian kingdom, one of about fifty royal houses whose inscriptions and whose sovereign claims extended over more than one of the linguistic, or cultural, regions of the peninsula from the time of the Chalukyas of Badami. Some sixty Vijayanagara rulers issued royal inscriptions claiming universal authority throughout the peninsula south of the Krishna River. In addition, there exist royal inscriptions of another twenty ruling families who acknowledged the overlordship of Vijayanagara kings, and another forty or so independent ruling families left inscriptions asserting sovereignty over some peninsular territory in the Vijayanagara age.

This multiplicity of sovereignties is very likely an underestimate, and it poses one set of confusions. Another arises from the fact that kings of Vijayanagara were of four distinct ruling lineages; they differed in language and provenance, in their religious affiliations and even in where their capitals were after the catastrophic sack of Vijayanagara in 1565. A beginning point in ordering that history is the founding of the fortified city on the Tungabhadra around 1340; a possibly earlier beginning point may well be the onset of the incursions of soldiers serving the Khalji sultans of Delhi, which allegedly created the reasons and conditions for the new dynasty and city of Vijayanagara.

THE GEOPOLITICAL PREHISTORY
OF VIJAYANAGARA

Krishnaswami Aiyangar postulated that the ordering principle of Vijayanagara history was to be a bastion against Islam, and he delineated the process generated by that principle. His *South India and her Muhammadan Invaders* outlined two separate histories

whose trajectories joined conjuncturally in the founding of Vijayanagara. One traced the fragmentation of the Chola political order
during the thirteenth century, the other the Khalji and Tughlak
invasions of the South during the fourteenth century.

By the beginning of the reign of Rajaraja III early in the thirteenth
century, Chola sovereignty had shrunk to a small portion of what
his namesake and real founder of the 'imperial' Cholas held at the
time of his death in 1016. The old core area of the kingdom –
Cholamandalam – was no longer under Rajaraja III's control. North
of the Kaveri, power had passed to several families of landed
magnates. One claiming descent from the ancient Pallavas ruled a
territory from the Kaveri to the Pennar River, near modern Madras;
to the north of that was another chiefdom claiming descent from the
Cholas themselves and ruling the delta of the Krishna and Godavari
Rivers; while yet another line of rulers, the Kakatiyas, claimed
hegemony over most of interior Telugu country. South of the
shrunken Chola core area was a revived Pandya kingship. All of
these rulers were rightly perceived by Krishnaswami Aiyangar as
contending authors of a new political integration in the South; and
in addition he referred to a large number of 'chieftains' from whom
little could be expected except political disorder as each sought to
expand against his neighbours. To this epoch of political reordering,
and drawn by it, came a new and vigorous Karnatak kingship, the
Hoysalas. Its fourth ruler, Vira Narasimha (reign 1220-38), established himself in the heart of Chola-Pandya country, at a place called
Kannanur near the Kaveri.

The prospect of victory by any of the principal actors in this
competition was thwarted by divisions within each of them; brother
fought brother among Pandyans (Sundara versus Vira Pandya) and
Cholas (Rajaraja III versus Rajendra III), and the two princely
brothers of the Hoysala Somesvara (reign 1233–67) divided Hoysala
authority between themselves, Ramanatha in Kannanur and Tamil
country and Narasimha III in Karnataka with his capital at Dvarasamudram, 200 miles away. Another aspect of diversity arose from
differences in form among the three major kingdoms of the southern
peninsula: Hoysalas in Karnataka, Kakatiyas in Andhra, and the
Chola and Pandya kingdoms of Tamil country. These differences
can be regarded as no more than tendencies now because they have

been little noted by South Indian historians, most of whom attribute a sameness to all Indian monarchies purporting to derive from ancient normative texts on government. However, changed conditions can be discerned, and these shaped the Vijayanagara kingdom of the fourteenth century and later.

Two factors are important: the resource bases of each of the three regional kingdoms and the geopolitical context in which each had to govern. The cores of the Hoysala and Kakatiya kingdoms lay respectively in the modern Hassan and Mandya districts of Karnataka and in Warangal district of Andhra. The resource bases of both can be assessed from conditions reported in the late eighteenth century and later. Both were in zones of low rainfall, receiving about 30 inches per year upon which crop production, and thus royal revenues, hazardously depended; in both realms the proportion of high agriculture based on irrigation was small, about one-fifth of sown acres in Hoysala domains and one-eighth in Kakatiya; in both also the ratio of cultivated to non-cultivated lands was relatively low, less than half. On agricultural grounds, thus, the central areas of both northern kingdoms were modest as compared with the Pandyas and Cholas.

The core territories of the latter nested within rich riverine basins providing extended zones of irrigated cultivation and thus more dense populations than could be sustained in the dry northern kingdoms. A territory like Tirunelveli, part of the Pandyan kingdom, was able to export grain, cotton, cotton cloth, and bullocks to the Malabar coast; the trade was balanced by the importation of money, coconuts, and fish into the principal core of Pandyan authority in the Vaigai basin at Madurai during the fourteenth century, according to the recent research of David Ludden. Even more, the Cholas were beneficiaries of extended exchange relations that reached to Malaysia, based on grain surpluses from the Kaveri. Thus, both Pandya and Chola kings could realise substantial revenue from agriculture as well as from trade that was available to neither Hoysalas nor Kakatiyas from within their domains. The central domains of the Pandyas and Cholas were treated as properties from which the ruling families of both extracted regular payments in kind and money.

Lacking such resources, the northern kingdoms undertook, on

the one hand, to establish and nurture trade centres which could exploit the slender commodity potentials of their domain and, on the other hand, to seize control of more established trade centres on their respective coasts. For them, conquest was an essential means of increasing the meagre resources they could command to meet the costs of warfare that this age entailed. An important indication of these differences in the scale and character of resources available and the strategies for their realisation to the respective kingdoms was the siting of their capitals.

The Hoysala capital until the late fourteenth century was Dvarasamudram, established in the hill-bounded area of modern Halebid in Hassan district by an eleventh-century Hoysala chief. Originally hill chiefs from the 5,000-foot highlands fifty miles west of Halebid, the Hoysalas moved from their hill fastness on to the neighbouring plains and replaced the fading overlordship of the Chalukyas of Kalyani. Their gradually expanding domain was protected by the fortified capital of Dvarasamudram set into the rock hills that extended from the northern highlands such as to effect a defensible frontier against the Chalukyas. Dvarasamudram was over twenty-five miles from the major area of agricultural production and settlement of the kingdom, on the Hemavati River, and forty-two miles north of the Kaveri, which formed the boundary with Gangavadi and its ancient Ganga kings to the south. Like the latter, the early Hoysalas were Jainas, and their capital became an important centre of Jainism (as was Talkad, the Ganga capital) until Hoysala Vishnuvardhana (reign 1110-52) converted to Vaishnavism, drove the Jainas from his capital, and built the distinctive temples to be seen at Halebid and Belur. By then too, the Hoysalas had become a dominant military power, adding to their realm by conquests that during the thirteenth century carried their authority to where the Kaveri delta began, between the centres of Chola and Pandya power in the south. There the second Hoysala capital Kannanur was established in the uplands over the gateway to the Kaveri delta where it resembled the capitals of other masters of river valleys more than it did Dvarasamudram and thus reflected the now divided character of the Hoysala kingdom.

The Kakatiya's Warangal was a twelfth-century capital as well. It was sited in a countryside even less prepossessing than Dvarasamudram and chosen for defence amongst great rocky outcrops and stony ridges. A great fortress was constructed there within whose walls there was extensive cultivation of dry crops. Irrigated cultivation was carried out at nearby Anamkonda, an earlier and less defensible capital and Jaina centre, where two large irrigation tanks existed. The Kakatiya captial, like the Hoysala one, was on a defensive frontier, whereas those of the Pandyas and Cholas were sited in the centre of the most valuable production for the most efficient management of their relatively greater resources.

The geopolitical context of the two northern kingdoms offers yet other explanations. The hill chieftains who established the Hoysala kingdom developed their military credentials during the twelfth century as paid soldiers under the older Karnataka kingdoms of the Kalyana Chalukyas and the Gangas. The centre of their new kingdom on the edge of the Karnataka plain had previously had no major political identity, being an area between two ancient territories – Banavasi and Nolambavadi in the north and Gangavadi in the south, the ancient Ganga kingdom. During the long reign of the Kalyana Chalukyan king, Vikramaditya (reign 1076–1126), the Hoysala chiefs began to be mentioned in inscriptions as subordinates who conquered the Ganga country and fought valiantly against the Cholas and other enemies of Vikramaditya. The Kakatiyas also set up their authority in an interstitial political zone and they, too, were involved with the Chalukyas of Kalyani. Kakatiya chiefs served under Chalukya Somesvara I when the latter campaigned in northern Andhra and attacked Kanchivaram and other places in northern Tamil country. By the late twelfth century, Kakatiya chiefs were issuing inscriptions of their own boasting of how they routed the Chalukya king Tailapa III (reign 1149-63). Both of the new kingdoms strove to establish their power along the rich trading coasts on opposite sides of the peninsula. The Kakatiyas extending their control from Telangana to the rich deltaic lands and ports of the Krishna-Godavarai delta; the Hoysalas, during the reign of Vishnuvardhana, seized the western coast from the Konkan, around Goa, south to Malabar. Both royal houses also expanded northward from their core territories, thereby setting a collision course with the southward expanding forces of the Delhi sultans during the fourteenth century.

MUSLIM INCURSIONS

The encounter with Muslim power from Delhi is perhaps the most important political fact of the period, as Krishnaswami Aiyangar and others have insisted. In the far south, Madurai was seized and brought under the Khalji sultanate in 1310, after their intervention in a civil war was sought by one of two warring Pandyan princes; Pandyan internecine fighting had already encouraged other interventions which weakened its authority, notably the invasion of the Travancore raja Ravivarman Kulasekhara. Further north, the Hoysala king, Vira Ballala III, was defeated and killed by Muslim soldiers of the breakway sultanate established at Madurai after he had reunited the kingdom previously divided between Tamil country and Karnataka by his father and uncle; later in 1329, soldiers of the Delhi sultan, Muhammad bin Tughlak, crushed the Kampili successors of the Hoysalas in Karnataka. Thus, within a remarkably brief period in the fourteenth century, all older centres of authority in the peninsula were obliterated by Muslim horsemen, leaving a vacuum that was to be filled by the able fighters who established Vijayanagara on the grave of the Kampili kingdom.

This was on the frontier where Muslim power at last took root in the middle of the peninsula, finding a permanent territorial base after fifty years of plundering. Between the short-lived Kampili kingdom and Vijayanagara were many links. Kampili was a mere twenty miles from where Vijayanagara was later established. The founder of Kampili, one Mummadi Singa, was, like the five sons of Sangama, a warrior in search of a territory to rule. In the case of Mummadi Singa, though, he was clearly a warrior from the hill country (*malnad*) of Karnataka, whereas the origin of the Vijayanagara founders remains uncertain. When the raja in whose service he was, Ramadevaraya of Devagiri, fell before the Muslims, Mummadi Singa fled south to the Tungabhadra where he established a strong fortress at Anegondi, in the same rocky outcrops along the Tungabhadra that shortly afterwards attracted the founders of Vijayanagara. From here, until his death in 1324, he won territories and followers from as far south as the Rayadurga, fifty miles away, and also imposed his authority over Raichur, north of the Tungabhadra, and even took Badami, seventy miles from his capital. His successor

Kampiladevaraya consolidated these conquests with the administrative assistance of Bukka, the son of Sangama, and with the military help of Bukka's four brothers who took service under Kampiladevaraya in campaigns into Telangana against the Kakatiyas. When the Delhi horsemen fell upon and killed Kampiladevaraya in 1327 it was ostensibly because the latter had chivalrously given shelter to one of the commanders of Muhammad bin Tughlak who quit the sultan's service. Raichur thereupon came under Muslim rule and remained the most serious issue of contention between the two states that succeeded to rule this portion of the central peninsula, Vijayanagara and the Bahmani sultans.

FOUNDING THE KINGDOM

Bukka and Harihara and the three other Sangama brothers in the service of Kampiladevaraya escaped from Anegondi when it was taken by Muhammad bin Tughlak's soldiers. Most historians of Karnataka claim that the brothers then took service under the Hoysala king Vira Ballala III. When the latter's capital of Dvarasamudram was in its turn sacked in 1327, Vira Ballala moved his court to Tiruvannamalai in northern Tamil country. At the same time, it is again supposed, Ballala established the fortified city on the Tungbhadra River across from Anegondi that was to become Vijayanagara. Among its several names then, the city was called Virupakshapattana (the town under the protection of Siva as the god Virupaksha whose shrine was there); this was intended to hold off further Muslim incursions into southern Karnataka. Bukka and Harihara were appointed to govern the new city according to these historians.

N. Venkataramanayya advanced a different possibility from documents of the seventeenth century purporting to prove that Harihara and Bukka had held important posts under Kakatiya Prataparudra, not Hoysala Vira Ballala. According to traditions he assembled, when Tughlak forces finally reduced the great fort at Warangal, the five sons of Sangama (Bukka, Harihara, Kampana, Mudappa, and Marappa) were made prisoners. They later converted to Islam and were employed by the sultan to govern the newly conquered Kampili territories. These persistent traditions plus others that refer to their later apostasy from Islam under the guidance of the famous savant and religious leader Madhavacharya, or Vidyaranya, and their establishment of a Hindu kingdom comprise the central mythical core of the origin of Vijayanagara.

Other elements of these origin accounts stress the incessant warfare among the numerous Hindu kingdoms of the peninsula which opened that territory to Muslim conquest. Ambitious warriors assumed royal titles and strove for dominance over kinsmen and neighbours; mobile warriors like the sons of Sangama roved the peninsula in quest of a territory to rule. All of this also forms part of the legend of Vijayanagara's foundation, and it applies as well to the ordinary political processes of later medieval South India. To view this disruption and competition as some sort of inter-imperial political chaos – as the disorder that followed the fall of older regimes such as Hoysalas and Kakatiyas or the Cholas and an anticipation of the new imperial order under Vijayanagara – posits a false telos. Fundamentally, the founding of Vijayanagara around 1340 occurred within and in response to a set of political processes that existed through much of the medieval era.

One factor, however, must be considered new – the fiercely expansive Muslim power of the fourteenth century. But even that is subject to the important qualification introduced by Krishnaswami Aiyangar, who was among the first to give Islam its critical place in Vijayanagara history. This was that Muslims had been part of South Indian society for a long time before Vijayanagara was founded. Muslim traders and even fighters were known on the Malabar coast from the tenth century. Arabs and other Muslims formed parts of the cosmopolitan trading communities found scattered along the whole western coast of India, and their presence along the eastern coast was recorded not much after the tenth century. Moreover, as early as the 1140s there are references to Muslim fighers employed by Hindu kings, such as the Hoysala king Jagademalla. These soldiers had no apparent connection with the Turkic warriors from Delhi who began their incursions into the South in the early fourteenth century.

The latter constituted a destructive element in the south for about half a century by amplifying an existing set of fissiparous forces within South Indian politics, though Turkic Muslims did not create the pervasive disorder of the age.

POLITICS AND ECOLOGY: THE
AGRARIAN FRONTIER

That was perhaps more the consequence of other processes, of which one was a shift of dominance in peninsular politics from the old riverine core kingdoms of the earlier medieval age to the large zone of upland, dry zone. Vijayanagara was to prove the grand apotheosis of this latter type of dominance.

Here, mixed rural economies of peasants, herdsmen, and forest people were the consequence of an age-long process of movement of an agricultural frontier from the ancient riverine cores to the watershed regions of the peninsula. In these areas of sparse rainfall, hardy peasant groups, prevented by insufficient water from achieving high levels of multi-crop production, were compelled to pursue plundering expeditions with fighting skills honed by turbulent relations with herdsmen and forest people. The Reddis and Velamas of Andhra and Vanniyars of Tamil country exemplify such warlike peasantries. Herdsmen, for their part, combined animal husbandry with dangerous long-distance trading, which was only possible using bullocks, and with plunder if trade was not possible. Finally, there were the hill and forest people who combined shifting cultivation with hunting and with raids upon peasants and herdsmen; their fighting skills were valued and purchased in the way that the founding chiefly family of the Hoysala kingdom, among others, have recounted of their forebears in their own genealogical accounts.

The opening of the extensive dry zone of the central peninsula – homelands of Hoysalas, Kakatiyas, and, later, Vijayanagara – was critically dependent upon tank irrigation. This was an agrarian technology whose antiquity reached back a millennium to Pallava and Chalukyan times and involved the bunding of low-lying lands to serve as catchments of rainfall and streams.

With the thirteenth-century Hoysalas and Kakatiyas, the ingredients for a more warlike age were at hand for peninsular societies. The superior cavalry and archery of Muslim fighters intensified this emerging martial quality, gave it an edge that doomed the older, more prosperous areas of agriculture and settlement in the river valleys to political subordination and plunder.

The early forays by the Khalji generalissimo Malik Kafur between 1290 and 1320 were probably more significant for northern India than for the South because the treasure from these plundering campaigns bought Delhi for Ala-ud-Din Khalji. However, Muhammad bin Tughlak's bold decision in 1328 to move his capital from Delhi to Devagiri brought Muslim power more dangerously close. Devagiri was the former capital of the Yadava kings of Maharashtra, (renamed Daulatabad): Muslim occupation there heralded a change in the conditions of Islamic power in the peninsula. Predation yielded to permanent domain, and Muslim influences upon a whole range of matters, including military ones, became more profound.

POLITICS AND THE NEW MILITARY

Contemporary documents confirm the impression among southern peoples that the Muslim horsemen from the North introduced a superior mode of cavalry warfare that both intensified military engagements and made them costlier. The ease with which small cavalry forces of sultanate soldiers brushed aside opponents points to the decisive edge in tactics and possibly in their *élan* as professional soldiers. Ala-ud-Din's first assault upon the peninsular kingdoms during the 1290s was at the head of 8,000 horsemen who crossed the Mahado Hills from around Gwalior to Devagiri, a distance of 400 miles, to win a treasure that helped to secure the Delhi throne for him. To succeed against such new foes required Hindu kings to imitate them: more and better horsemen and stronger fortresses. During the Tughlak era in the South, Hindu kings were compelled to have a core of soldiers in their permanent employ in order to field forces with more technical abilities than Hindu armies were required to have in the past. To cope with the large and mobile cavalry forces of the sultans, a Hindu ruler had to have similar force even if for longer campaigns he had to depend upon the levies of local chiefs. The provision of cavalry mounts, the expense of their maintenance and that of the fighters who used them was a heavy, new financial charge upon Hindu rulers. War elephants were another, and the latter became among the most valuable prizes of warfare and a reason for Hindu kings to have control of, or good relations with, forest chiefdoms where elephants were captured and trained for work or fighting.

Other evidence refers to the growing number of fighters seeking military employment in the peninsula, among them Sangama and his sons. The reported standing of Bukka and Harihara derived from their prowess as soldiers. Military careers offered ever wider choices of employers, and these increased for any fighter who converted to Islam. While being a Muslim did not confer equality with the great Turkic commanders, it did nevertheless open great careers. An example was the Khalji commander Malik Kafur, a Gujarati convert to Islam, who held the view that Muslim soldiers serving Hindu kings whom he captured should not be killed because they could at least repeat the credo. Thus, being a Muslim did confer standing for any man in a society becoming more urban under Muslim pressures.

When Muhammad bin Tughlak decided to establish his capital in Maharashtra, he ordered Delhi citizens to trek the 500 miles to it. This notorious act is but an extreme manifestation of the urban-centredness of all Muslim regimes in India. Accordingly, it has proved pointless to attempt to analyse the administrative control of the southern countryside under the Tughlaks, because there was no such control. Great commanders were granted *iqta* holdings nominally assignments of land revenue for their maintenance, by the sultan, but such grants never became reliable sources of income either to a sultan or to his assignees during the fourteenth century, if they ever did. When Muslim power struck roots in the peninsula, it was in cities, even if, as in the case of Muhammad bin Tughlak, these had to be 'imported' from elsewhere. Cities provided military security and commercial wealth and became the nodes of Muslim power and settlement; where the mosque was established the moral centre of society existed and being a Muslim meant superior standing.

DESTRUCTION OF THE OLD ORDER:
TOWNS, TEMPLES AND COMMERCE

Under the changing conditions of the fourteenth century – a more professionalised military that offered great careers to Muslim soldiers and hastened urbanisation – an ancient Indian conception of polity came under threat. This was the idea underpinning the segmentary political forms of the Chola age and earlier that assumed that political authority was shared between great kings and local, landed lordships – the idea of *dayada*. That this conception was not wholly displaced, any more than the segmentary forms with which it was associated, is clear from the seventeenth-century Marathi treatise on polity by Banahatti, *Ajnapatra*. According to this text that had currency during the age of Maratha supremacy in India, the small, self-sufficient chiefs of the countryside, deceptively regarded as 'office-holders', in reality were sharers of royal sovereignty. Such a conception of sovereignty was weakened by Muslim rulers under whom local Hindu lordships were wholly suspect and for whom such a notion of sharing was as morally unacceptable as it was normative for Hindus. But such a weakening provided a new basis for post-Muslim kingdoms of the south, and most especially that of Vijayanagara.

The corroding effect of urbanisation upon the old order was not merely set by military and political factors; temples were another cause. By late medieval times, when state building and tank building had become a single process, both were additionally linked to the raising of temple towns. The pre-Vijayanagara age saw developments in temple construction that have become canonical in Indian art history. Equally well recognised now by economic historians is the important role of temples in their often extensive rural hinterlands. During the late, pre-Vijayanagara age, money and lands were gifted to temples to support priests and others upon whom worship, administration and care of temples depended. A common method of resource management by temple authorities with large landholdings was the deployment of money endowments as investments in irrigation works in 'temple villages' in order to increase the income upon which temples had a claim.

By an interrelated combination of political and religious investments, therefore, many places in the dry peninsula developed microzones of high agriculture based on tank irrigation and often upon the production of cash crops like cotton and indigo. The proliferation of such microzones resulted from the same investment practices being followed in smaller temples as well as larger ones, and by great and small chiefs. All contributed to transforming the dry upland interior of the peninsula from a zone of marginal agriculture and animal rearing into a zone of robust, mixed agriculture capable of supporting increasing numbers of people and more elaborate social and political institutions. And as with frontier societies elsewhere, those of the peninsular upland were led by fighting chiefs and its people trained and accustomed to fighting for their new lands. The Vijayanagara kingdom of the fourteenth century was a major beneficiary of this long process of development, and, in their turn, its rulers lent support to it.

Another prior development from which the Vijayanagara kingdom benefited was a commercial resource of almost unlimited potential based upon expanding international trade from the coasts of the peninsula. While the military impact of Muslims upon South India and Vijayanagara has been a fixture of Vijayanagara historiography for over a century, the simultaneous commercial impact is still too recent as a subject to have been assimilated to most interpretations of Vijayanagara. How recent this is may be judged from the significance accorded to K. N. Chaudhuri's *Trade and Civilization in the Indian Ocean; An Economic History from the Rise of Islam to 1750*, published in 1985.

The west coast of India was part of a system of 'emporia trade' that stretched over the whole of what Chaudhuri called 'the zone of Islamic influence'. This reached from the Atlantic coasts of Iberia and West Africa to the Indonesian archipelago and China and was defined by two trade modes, an overland caravan route and a sea route. The latter began in the Mediterranean and consisted of trade centres from the Arabian peninsula to India's western coast, to Malacca, and to southern China. This oceanic network had come into existence around AD 1000 replacing more hazardous single voyages from the Arabian core of the Islamic world to China which prevailed from the eighth to the eleventh centuries. According to Chaudhuri, the shaping force was political: the coalescence of two great political orders at opposite ends of the Eurasian world, which he dates in the early seventh century with the establishment of the T'ang dynasty in China and the flight of the Prophet Muhammad from Mecca to Medina: 'Separate and unconnected events mark out a fresh beginning, a new order.'

The seventh-century China-Near Eastern conjuncture was to be followed by a second around the year 1000. Then, China was ruled by an expansive Sung dynasty, and the Arabic successors of the prophet had become absorbed into the ancient political formation of the Near East, now revitalised by Islam under the Baghdadi Abbasid caliphs continuing an Islamic expansion that profoundly altered the late medieval Indian world, its warfare, politics, and commerce.

Everywhere in the Islamic world after AD 1000, there was the growth of urban centres spurred by political integration and nurtured by new concentrations of administrative-military élites with high consumption demands. This 'universal feature of Islam', in Chaudhuri's terms, stimulated international trade. When the Abbasid regime was swept away by Central-Asian Muslim Turks and by Mongols during the twelfth and thirteenth centuries, this added to the military superiority of Islam without diminishing the forces of economic expansion. Turks and Mongols were assimilated to the prevailing Muslim political and economic order and in the end fortified it militarily.

By AD 1500, there were numerous entrepôts from East Africa to Japan, the tempo of whose commerce was fixed by monsoonal winds which set the timings of all sailings; and of the four major commodities of this world trade-system, two – sandalwood and pepper – were contributed by India. As early as the tenth century, Chaudhuri shows, products from the eastern Mediterranean region and those from China met on India's western coast where sandalwood and pepper of Indian provenance were added. Thirteenth-century writings of the Sung official Chan Ju-Kua, Jewish merchants in western India whose letters were found in the Cairo Genizah, Marco Polo's narrative, and Ibn Battuta's travel account of the early fourteenth century all document India's place in this world trade and provide contemporary descriptions of many of the Indian emporia. They also took some notice at least of interior urban centres whose consumption demands buoyed up the coastal emporia.

Another stimulus to south Indian urbanisation came from Hindu temples. Many temple complexes served as political capitals, and others which received royal largesse often afforded occasional shelter to kings of the pre-Vijayanagara age as they progressed their realms; at Hindu shrines, kings received tribute of which part was deployed as gifts to Indian gods in return for which they received royal honours from their priests. Moreover, large temple centres, with their high walls and lofty gateways, were major military centres and protected places of commerce associated with pilgrims. For all these reasons, when Vira Ballala III was driven from Dvarasamudram in 1327, he took refuge in the Siva temple-centre of Tiruvannamalai in northern Tamil country. And the first generation of Vijayanagara rulers established their moral, or dharmic, claims to kingship by their publicised protection of Hindu shrines from the desecration of Muslims.

THE EARLY VIJAYANAGARA KINGDOM

Under these early kings, Vijayanagara became an empire in the sense of exercising rule over regions and peoples of the peninsula who were of different languages and cultures. They accomplished this principally by conquests over lesser Hindu lordships – kingdoms and chiefdoms – and by defending their conquests against the sultanate founded immediately to the north by Ala-ud-Din Gangu Bahmani about a decade after Vijayanagara was established. The Bahmani capital was at Gulbarga in Karnataka and its first war against Vijayanagara was launched from there in 1347; thereafter warfare betweeen the two was frequent. However, when the founding Vijayanagara dynasty began to experience its most severe difficulties during the late fifteenth century, it was as a result of internal dissensions rather than external pressures. These difficulties were resolved only after two usurpations at the turn of the sixteenth century which brought the Tuluva dynasty to the throne. Under them, Vijayanagara authority and glory were revived to a condition exceeding anything before, especially under Krishnadevaraya (reign 1509–29). In the remaining pages of this chapter, the history of the first, or Sangama, dynasty will be outlined.

Harihara ruled as king first and was followed by his old companion in arms and office, his brother Bukka. The other three Sangama brothers each had a portion of the kingdom to conquer and govern, and each ruled with a degree of independence that prompted Venkataramanayya to observe: 'Vijayanagara was more a group of semi-autonomous states than a unified kingdom.' The fragmented state was unified under Bukka's son, of the second generation of Vijayanagara kings, who ruled as Harihara II (1377–1404). Centralised authority was enhanced by the occasional appointment of non-kinsmen, including Brahmans, to important military commands, and even to governorships of one of the five core provinces (rajya, i.e. the king's) in the centre of the kingdom. But this was not the usual policy; most often sons of the king ruled for him as Harihara's son, Devaraya, did at the great fortress of Udayagiri in Telugu country from where attacks against the dominant local lords there were launched.

The most important of the latter were the Reddi kings of Kondavidu, and it was Devaraya's purpose to drive them from their territories south of the Krishna, hoping to make that river the north-eastern frontier of Vijayanagara. Devaraya's campaign dragged on for twenty-five years, a tribute to the stubborn fortitude of the professedly peasant Reddi kings of Kondavidu and also other peasant chieftains of the Velama caste of eastern Telangana. The Reddis and Velmas not only resisted the extension of Vijayanagara authority into their lands, but made common cause with the Bahmanis as well. Thus, attempts to set the north-eastern frontier of the kingdom was attended by bloody turmoil and a legacy of distrust and opposition that was to plague the kingdom to its final days.

To the south and west, conquests were more successful. Under Bukka I (reign 1344–77), Madurai was freed from the control of Muslim rebel commanders who declared a sultanate independent of the Tughlaks in 1334. The Vijayanagara campaign against them was carried out between 1365 and 1370 by Bukka I's son Kumara Kampana and was as much a propaganda as military success because it was memorialised in numerous inscriptions over the southern peninsula proclaiming a new dharmic kingship and an end to Muslim oppression. Another of Bukka I's sons, who was ruler as Harihara II (1377–1404), sought to impose the authority of Vijayanagara over the commercially important Malabar coast, displacing a brief Bahmani overlordship from Goa to Chaul, near modern Bombay. In the north-west, the River Krishna did become the frontier of Vijayanagara as a result of wars with the Bahmani which yielded control of the Raichur tract north of their capital.

Devaraya I (reign 1406–24) returned to the scenes of his wars as a prince in the north-east and was again opposed by the Reddis of Kondavidu and the Velamas of Warangal who allied themselves with the Bahmanis when necessary and also with the Hindu Gajapati kings of Orissa. The latter became an increasingly menacing force during the fifteenth century, extending their power into Telangana and coastal Andhra and even into Tamil country when any weakness or preoccupation of the Vijayanagara kings permitted, as after the death of Devaraya II in 1446, the last strong king of the Sangama line.

Devaraya II's Vijayanagara was impressive. He succeeded in winning the Velamas over from their Reddi and Bahmani allies and with their help defeated the Gajapatis, though that eastern region remained a troubled one. His successors were more lasting elsewhere, as in his reassertion of Vijayanagara dominance over the commercially important western coast. Much of his success came as a result of having recruited Muslim soldiers into his armies, by conferring high posts and rewards upon them and by constructing a mosque in Vijayanagara. Devaraya also improved the quality of his cavalry by controlling Malabar ports through which horses from Arabia passed. In addition to all of this, his court was famed for its brilliant literary circle in which the king was a participating maker of Sanskrit verse and whose most celebrated member was the Telugu poet Srinatha.

After his death, the Orissan Gajapatis, who had fared badly in their wars against him, launched a powerful counterattack against Vijayanagara authority in Andhra. This the Gajapatis now claimed for themselves, and they also drove all Vijayanagara authority from the Tamil plain north of the Kaveri by seizing Tiruchirappalli. To this humiliation lethal rivalries among members of the royal line were added, which permitted power to pass to the trusted commander, Saluva Narasimha. He defended the kingdom until the late years of the fifteenth century when he murdered the last of the Sangamas and established himself as king. When Narasimha died in 1491, he left a young son as the ward of his favourite general, a warrior from Tulu country on the western coast, Narasa Nayaka. The latter in his turn seized the throne at Vijayanagara, thus inaugurating the third dynasty of the kingdom, called the Tuluva.

The decline that began after the reign of Devaraya II had many causes. Velamas were forced by Bahmani expansion into Telangana to move their power southward into Kurnool where they clashed with chiefs under a Vijayanagara protection which could not be fulfilled. The Bahmanis had begun by now to concert their attacks against Vijayanagara with the Gajapatis led by their warrior king Kapiladeva. But the major cause of Vijayanagara decline was dissension among claimants to the throne and their machinations, which finally induced Saluva Narasimha, the military saviour of the dynasty in its last years, to seize power. He was to be a bridge into a new political phase of Vijayanagara history.

THREE

THE CITY AND THE KINGDOM

The city was known by several names besides 'Vijayanagara', which is hardly surprising since the earliest inscription from the place in Brahmi script dates from about the second century. From the eleventh to the thirteenth centuries, several other inscriptions are found, including one registering gifts made to the temple of the goddess Hampadevi (or Pampadevi) from which the modern village on the ruins of the city, Hampi, presumably comes. Hoysala-period inscriptions refer to the place as Virupakshapattana or Vijaya Virupakshapura in honour of the god Siva, as Virupaksha, protector of the large settlement the place had become in the fourteenth centruy. These pre-Vijayanagara references make it clear that the future capital of the Vijayanagara kingdom was one of the many places in modern Bellary with a past history dating to Mauryan times when Ashokan edicts were inscribed within thirty miles of Hampi, along banks of the Tungabhadra.

Seventy-seven inscriptions of the Vijayanagara age itself have been discovered around Hampi. Most (sixty-five) are found inscribed on temples along the banks of the Tungabhadra; the balance are in parts of the city that were added during the massive constructions of the sixteenth century by kings of the Tuluva dynasty. Fully half of the inscriptions found on the riverside were on the Vithala shrine. The temples upon whose walls and basements most inscriptions are found display a cosmopolitan character befitting an imperial capital. Stylistic variety and other cultural features of the ruins at Hampi have been carefully analysed during the remarkable efflorescence of Vijayanagara studies that began in the 1970s, to which valuable contributions have come from foreign as well as Indian scholars. Among the former is the architectural historian George Michell, who has documented something of the variety of styles in the built environment of Hampi.

He and others delineate three broad zones within the walled capital city. One extends along the Tungabhadra bank and has been called 'the sacred centre' of the city; a second broad zone is called 'the urban core'. This part of the Hampi site is designated as 'the royal centre', on which no pre-Vijayanagara structures have been found. The sacred centre and urban core, with its royal centre, are separated from each other by an irrigation canal that defines an intervening agricultural zone of Hampi as shown on Map 3.

Since the 'royal centre' includes some sixty ruined temples, the designations 'sacred' and 'royal' should not be taken as rigorous categories of built space and function in the city. Among the oldest shrines in the 'royal centre' is a second dedicated to the god Virupakasha in the city, the other being the larger and older temple on the river. Michell and others believe that the smaller, fourteenth-century Virupaksha shrine may have served as a royal chapel; it displays many elements of temple architecture found north of the Tungabhadra and is thus designated as 'Deccan style'. Most smaller shrines in this southern part of the Hampi site display a similar Deccani style. However, with the fifteenth-century Ramachandra temple in the royal centre elements of 'southern style' appear. These were derived from late Chola and Pandya temples first seen during fourteenth-century conquests. 'Southern' or 'Dravidian' architectural elements were adapted to older Deccani ones by adding such distinctive features as high-walled enclosures forming interior walkways around an often older central shrine, pillared halls, sculpted basements, and, most distinctively of all, towering gateways set into the high walls.

The best examples of temple building in the sixteenth-century heyday of Vijayanagara are found in the northern section of Hampi, the 'sacred centre' along the riverside. Here are found complete temple complexes dedicated to Virupaksha, Balakrishna, Tiruvengalanatha (the god Venkatesvara from Tirupati or 'Achyutadevaraya's temple'), Vithala, Ragunatha, and Pattibhirama. These several shrines manifest – indeed they constitute – the first examples of what art historians call the Vijayanagara temple style, one that spread widely with the conquests of the Tuluva kings during the sixteenth century.

Excavations in the vicinity of these several temple complexes now permit a better understanding of why each seemed to have a somewhat separate and independent identity in inscriptions. The precincts of the old, riverside shrine of Virupaksha in the north-western part of Hampi was called Virupakshapura in an inscription of

Hoysala Ballala III; the environs of the Krishna shrine, north of the dividing irrigation canal, was known as Krishnapura. That the designation 'pura', or 'city', was more than a conceit honouring the god whose temple formed the focus of the quarter is indicated by recent excavations. Fronting all of the principal temples were long, paved roads. The road in front of the riverside Virupaksha temple extends for one-half mile and along its sides are structures of various sorts, some probably being public buildings, perhaps audience halls, and others being shops and residences of merchants. A sixteenth-century inscription refers to the road beginning in front of the Ramachandra temple as 'big bazaar street'.

Domingo Paes's description of the city in 1520 retains remarkable freshness; it is also one whose accuracy is validated by each new excavation at the Hampi site. Paes entered the city by its western gate:

> The king has made within it a very strong city, fortified with walls and towers, and the gates at the entrance are very strong ... these walls are not made like those of other cities, but are made of very strong masonry ... and inside very beautiful rows of buildings ... with flat roofs. There live ... many merchants, and it is filled with a large population because the king induces many honourable merchants to go there from his cities ...[1]

Not far from the western gate was the Ramachandra temple, before which, Paes reported:

> You have a broad and beautiful street full of fine houses ... and it is understood that the houses belong to ... merchants, and there you find all sorts of rubies, and diamonds, and emeralds, and pearls ... and cloths and every sort of thing there is on the earth that you may wish to buy. Then you have there every evening a fair where they sell many common horses, and also many citrons, and limes, and oranges, and grapes, and every kind of garden stuff, and wood; you have all this in the street [which] ... leads to the palace.[2]

There was found the king, Krishnadevaraya, who was

> of medium height, and of fair complexion and good figure, rather fat than thin; he has on his face signs of smallpox. He is the most

[1] R. Sewell, *A Forgotten Empire (Vijayanagara)* (London: Sonnenswahnheim, 1900), p. 244; Delhi edition, 1962: p. 236
[2] Sewell, *Forgotten Empire*, London edition: pp. 246–7; Delhi edition: p. 239

feared and perfect king that could possibly be ... He is a great ruler
and a man of much justice ...[3]

Archaeological findings have confirmed inscriptions and Indian
literary evidence as well as the accounts of foreigners who visited the
city before and after Paes. As a result of all of this, the city can be
understood more clearly than ever before.

Its northern flank was the Tungabhadra on whose north bank
were defensive walls anchored on the east by the fortress and town
of Anegondi. This fortified town was constructed by the Kampili
kings of the fourteenth century, and their defensive walls reached
northward into the Raichur countryside. South-west of Anegondi,
on the south bank of the river, is 'the sacred centre' of Vijayanagara,
where, strung along the Tungabhadra, like so many jewels, are the
remarkable temple complexes. These are nested into small valleys
that break the rocky ridgeline which follows the southern bank of
the Tungabhadra.

Immediately south of this broken riverside ridge lies an extensive
irrigated, agricultural zone defined by a shallow valley that was
probably an ancient course of the river to which it is even now
opened on both of its ends. The canal still passes through this valley
and makes it a verdant zone of irrigated cultivation; the canal
receives water from the river through each of the small valleys that
breach the ridge and provide the settings for each temple complex.
Ancient bridges cross the canal, connecting two major roads that
pass from the southern parts of Hampi – 'the urban core' – to the
river.

South of the agricultural zone, the landscape changes only slightly
to open onto a broken flat area, studded with massive boulders and
rock outcrops that were ingeniously incorporated into an intricate
series of defensive walls within which nested other wall-enclosed
structures. Here, in 'the urban core', are found the remains of wells,
tanks, pottery, and other signs that this was the place where most of
Vijayanagara's citizens lived. Among these were Muslim soldiers
and artisans who served the kings of the sixteenth century and who
were permitted mosques and tombs and cemeteries. Remains of all
of these are found on the eastern edge of the urban core of the

---

[3] Sewell, *Forgotten Empire*, London edition: pp. 255–6; Delhi edition: pp. 246–7.

Hampi site as well as in two of the southern suburbs of the city, Kamalapuram and Kadirampur. These Muslim-style structures seem to date from the early fifteenth century, and one, a mosque, has an inscription dating the building from 1439.

What scholars of the city are calling 'the royal centre' lies in the western half of the urban and residential core south of the irrigation canal. Here are the largest and possibly the earliest extant remains of what can be called 'civil monuments' in South India in the sense that these structures which were not the shelter of gods and institutions of religious activity. Another defining characteristic of the royal centre is a system of roads, many stone-paved, radiating outward from an open area in front of the Ramachandra temple and reaching all parts of the site south of the agricultural zone and a few of these extending northward to the Tungabhadra banks.

In the capitals of the Cholas, Pandyas, and Hoysalas – Tanjavur and Gangaikondacholapuram, Madurai, and Dvarasamumdram – were large temples, and some may have served as the residences of kings. But in Vijayanagara there are the remains of imposing secular buildings which match the detailed descriptions of Paes and another Portuguese traveller, Fernão Nuniz, who was there in 1535. Thirty or so 'palaces' have now been identified in various parts of the city. Most are in the south-western portion, or the royal centre, and several have been fully excavated. One set of these structures is found north of the irrigation canal, and in it has been found a large number of Chinese porcelain pieces, possibly brought from the west coast ports where Chinese commodities were reportedly exchanged for commodities from India and the Near East. The largest of these 'palace' buildings so far found is south of the canal and covers an area of 7,700 square feet, not including its walls. The idea that these buildings were shelters for royals and other important residents of the city is based partly upon the evidence of Paes, Nuniz, and other fifteenth- and sixteenth-century visitors, partly on their inappropriateness as religious buildings, and partly also on the evidence that in them household-scale cooking went on and some rooms may have served as offices. The largest number of extant great houses are found in close proximity to the Ramachandra temple and near a set of other ceremonial structures which are certainly the same ones described by Paes, Nuniz, and others as where the great royal festival, called Mahanavami or Dassara, was performed.

Among the most striking of all of Hampi's ruined structures are those where royal ceremonials were conducted. While these structures contain architectural and iconographic elements commonly found on temples of the time, there were no cells in which the images of gods could be placed and worshipped nor are these structures oriented appropriately. Some of these 'civic' buildings possess structural elements that provide for substantial wooden and cloth superstructures of a sort described by foreign visitors. One of these has a floor area of 5,300 square feet rising by a series of sculpted terraces to some 40 feet above a base measuring 11,700 square feet. This 'great platform', or 'mahanavami dibba' as the modern residents of Hampi call it, is a remarkable structure which during the sixteenth century was surmounted by another level supported by wooden columns. It is probable that the platform dated from the fourteenth century and therefore that many of Vijayanagara's rulers received the homage and their tutelaries the worship of their subjects before the time of Krishnadevaraya when the final layers of sculpted panels are thought to have been affixed.

Close to the great platform the ruins of encircling walls and of elaborate tanks and aqueducts are found. Among these an exquisitely constructed, large step well has recently been excavated, in a design heretofore seen primarily in southern Maharashtra, thus extending the symbolic reach of this City of the Rayas. Also near the platform other important structures have been found. One of these has a floor area twice as large as the 'dibba'. This is a hall in whose floor extending over 17,000 square feet are footings for one hundred columns to support another storey connected to the first by a stone stairway that still stands. This must be the building mentioned by the horse trader and emissary Abdar Razzaq during his visit to the city in 1442–3 and which he called 'the royal audience hall'. Another notable recent find is a set of dressed stone slabs that appear to have been brought to the city for use in sixteenth-century constructions from early Buddhist sites in northern Karnataka.

The designation by site archaeologists of many of the ruined structures as 'palaces' departs from their otherwise prudent practice of not attributing functions to particular structures as older scholars of the site did when whole sections of the site were identified as bureaucratic offices, such as a 'mint'. There is no evidence that such offices existed. The attribution of 'palace' to some of these buildings may be justified, however, and other sets of structures may also justifiably be said to have had public functions.

One such cluster is in an area north of the great platform of the royal centre. It consists of a set of buildings that are so well preserved and have such markedly Muslim features that some earlier commentators have proposed that they may have dated from after the sack of the city in 1565. One of these is a two-storeyed pavilion long called the 'lotus mahal' which is richly decorated with Hindu and Muslim elements, thus adding to the new and eclectic architecture identified with Vijayanagara. Within the same walled enclosure other notable buildings in the same style are discovered. These include a building with eleven domes that was almost certainly an elephant stable, another was an arched building still preserved, that may have served as a 'guards' quarters', and in an adjoining enclosure there is a water pavilion which may have served as a royal bath and was earlier called 'the queen's bath'. The notion that these are creations of the post-1565 life of the city is not accepted by art and architectural historians.

Secular or civil buildings of the royal centre south of the agricultural zone of the city, together with the temple complexes in the northern sector of the Hampi site, give an expressive, or emblematic, character to the whole of Hampi that is most manifest in the annual ten-day Mahanavami Festival, conducted during the lunar month of Asvina (September/October). Celebrated in this rite were the victories, powers, and protection of the tutelary goddess of the kings, the apotheosis of perfect kingship as symbolised by the god Rama, and the puissance and protection of all of the gods and people 'of the world' by the Vijayanagara kings who were the focus of the festival. This annual, royal rite was probably the most important ceremony that occurred in the city during its two centuries as a great capital, and it serves as a means of understanding the relationship among some of the key structures of the royal centre, especially the Ramachandra temple, the great platform, and the hundred-pillared hall. All are mentioned in the descriptions of the Mahanavami Festival by sixteenth-century visitors to the city.

In turn, all of this leads to the question of what the city tells us of the kingdom and 'empire' in whose name they have been known to historians.

This is not an easy question to answer. For instance, if the triage sometimes used to categorise pre-modern cities is applied to Vijayanagara, the outcome is so ambiguous as to cast doubt upon the categories themselves. Vijayanagara was a regal-ritual centre *and* an administrative centre *and* a commercial centre: it was these and more.

It certainly was a royal city and one in which ritual was very important in at least two ways. Temples of the so-called sacred centre were replete with divine and royal potency. The goddess Pampa, consort of Siva, continued to be protector of the city and its kings even under the post-Sangama rulers who were personally devoted to such Vishnu deities as Krishna and Tiruvengalanatha for whom temples were built by Krishnadevaraya and Achyutadevaraya, and the Rama temple of the royal centre was the focus of the royal rituals of both. The Balakrishna image installed in a new temple by Krishnadevaraya was both his personal god and a trophy of his prowess in having seized the image from Udayagiri when that fortress was taken from the Gajapatis in 1515. Achyutadevaraya's temple to Tiruvengangalnatha similarly honours the personal god of the king (i.e. Venkatesvara) and celebrates his coronation before that god in 1529 under very troubled conditions. The Vithala temple begun by Devaraya II was possibly the most popular temple of the sixteenth century and remains one of the most beautiful temples in all of India. Curiously, this manifestation of Vishnu is better known in Maharashtra than in Karnataka or further south and therefore may take note of Krishnadevaraya's northern conquests. Hence, all of the great shrines of Vijayanagara, including that of Virupaksha, in one way or another, ritually focussed upon powerful royal benefactors; the regal and the ritual constituting as powerful a composite for the Vijayanagara kings as for most other Indian kings. As a ritual or ceremonial centre, the city was a greatly enlarged, yet unified, version of the Chalukyan royal centres of Aihole and Pattadakal, according to the descriptions and poetry of contemporaries and to what can be beheld by the modern sojourner at Hampi.

But Vijayanagara was also an important commercial centre. It was the focal point of several transpeninsular trade routes, and the commodities which found their way to the city impressed Portuguese visitors of the sixteenth century by their variety and quality. Wares would have been seen at the four large bazaars that were said to exist in the royal centre alone; in addition, each of the temple complexes along the river had a bazaar street whose trade, along with that of the several southern suburbs of the city, was conducted by the merchant guilds of each. All of this together with the vivid descriptions by Paes and Nuniz of the trade that had lured them to the city, make Vijayanagara a thriving emporium and production centre. And, of course, it was a centre of vast consumption as the administrative centre of a great kingdom.

Vijayanagara was the place where its kings conducted their political business for substantial parts of each year, where tribute from powerful provincial lords of the realm was received during the mahanavami festival, and where the rayas' army was garrisoned and resupplied when it was not in the field. Foreign commentators documented all of these activities. Among the earliest, Nicolo di Conti reported that the city accommodated an army of 90,000 in 1420, and later fifteenth-century witnesses referred to even larger numbers of soldiers who were garrisoned and otherwise cared for there. Nuniz listed the great commanders of these and other forces of the kingdom from whom Achyutadevaraya received substantial tribute payments in gold coins. While there were said to be some two hundred of these 'captains of his kingdom', Nuniz recorded the tribute received from only eleven, and he stated the territories of each. These tributaries paid the king between a third and a half of their money collections, retaining the balance to support their own armed forces. Nuniz observed that Achyutadevaraya employed officials to record and collect the revenues from lands around the city – 'the King's own lands' – but that there were no royal officials responsible for the general revenues of the kingdom.

FISCAL BASIS OF THE KINGDOM

The modest assessment of Vijayanagara state administration set out by Paes and Nuniz, and accepted by Robert Sewell, has not been contravened by later historians, nor by the excavations being conducted at the Hampi site. For instance, the large enclosure within the royal centre that was designated as the 'mint' by earlier historians (most of whom had never visited Hampi) has been rejected partly because there are no material traces of minting and partly because the ruined structures of most of the walled enclosures are now thought to have been residential quarters – 'palaces' – on somewhat better, though still slender, evidence. There is an underground chamber in the royal centre that may have served as a treasury, but this merely underscores the modest character of administrative functions in the city. What other administrative functions might have been present in sixteenth-century Vijayanagara has something to do with how the political structure of the kingdom is viewed.

As already noted, historians of Karnataka and Andhra perceive no differences between the Vijayanagara regime and its predecessors, nor do they admit of changes in the kingdom from the time of its founding until, possibly, the sacking of the city in 1565; some do not even regard that event as an important turning-point. Tamil historians, however, see Vijayanagara differently, if only in the sense that the Tamils ceased to be subjugators of other peninsular people and became the subjugated. But even this reversal is not seen by most older Tamil historians as more important than the vaunted role of Vijayanagara kings as defenders of southern dharma from Muslim desecrations.

The recent research findings of N. Karashima and Y. Subbarayalu are important departures from the older historiography in several ways. They proceed from a perspective of the pre-Vijayanagara state and society, and they make significant temporal comparisons as well as being explicitly concerned to stipulate and to theorise the connections between the Vijayanagara state and the local lordships with which their evidence deals. Karashima at times adopts a feudal interpretation of Vijayanagara, one that is focussed upon relations between kings and local lordships, emphasising the following elements: personal and fealty affinities, a notion of fief attributed to landholding terms such as *sirmai* and *nayakattana*; the appearance of what he calls sub-infeudation among nayakas; and the complex landholding rights of Vijayanagara times as compared with the communal unity of the Chola period. However, these sorts of relations are not claimed for Tamil country until the sixteenth century. Before that the picture presented by Karashima and others in unclear. It seems to be that during the fifteenth century, Vijayanagara soldiers are seen to be agents of a conquest state, charged with extracting a large money revenue from the conquered Tamils, and producing peasant resistance against the extortionate demands of these military agents and their Brahman and Tamil landlord allies.

Relations between local lordships and Vijayanagara kings – whether seen as feudal or other – cannot be verified except from local documents of the sort studied by Karashima, Subbarayalu, and others. Hence, the discussion of this political dimension will be treated in the following chapter. Here, the broader history of the Vijayanagara kingdom and its political structure will be outlined.

Two fundamental changes seem to have occurred around the time of Devaraya II, in the middle of the fifteenth century. First, he strengthened the military base of the kingdom by improving the quality of war horses and the training of horsemen and archers under his personal command and resources, and, second, he established deeper political control over west-coast emporia, thus linking military reform with international commerce.

Military and administrative dominance over the major ports on the Arabian Sea provided Devaraya II with a new and different source of state finance that his predecessors ever enjoyed, though exactly how trade profits were appropriated during the fifteenth century cannot now be ascertained. Fifty years later, there is some evidence to suggest that a standard means of realising revenue was through tax-farming, though whether tax-farmers were agents of the rayas or of other imperial grandees is uncertain. Nevertheless, contemporary inscriptions and later literary sources document that in addition to older forms of tax in kind, especially on the production of grain and some cash crops, there was added a whole set of cash revenue demands. The latter were collected from trade and from the production of textiles and metal goods either from the headmen of artisanal groups or traders or by contracting out, or farming, revenue collections to men with independent military and political powers and authority and sometimes to merchants directly involved in trade. Customs collections at major trade centres were let on rent agreements (or *gutta*) from powerful, state-level magnates, often with close relations to reigning kings of Vijayana-gara. Nuniz, for example, reported in 1535 that the annual collection of customs from one of the gateways of Vijayanagara was rented for 12,000 gold coins. While a full range of taxes collected during the fifteenth century is not retrievable, customs, or tribute paid by merchants, from port towns in the time of Devaraya II could have provided the means for him to pay for horses imported from Ormuz and elsewhere as well as providing a surplus to pay for the skilled horsemen to use them.

Saluva Narasimha continued Devaraya's policy of making larger appropriations where possible from west-coast emporia and went further by attempting to achieve the same in Coromandel. By seizing direct control over the northern Coromandel plain and extirpating those conquered regimes that had previously been left in place on condition of accepting the supremacy of Vijayanagara, potential central resources were increased. The initial Vijayanagara conquests under Kumara Kampana during the late fourteenth century merely demanded the homage of the Sambuvaraya chief of Tondaimandalam and that of the royal houses of Cholas and Pandyas. This practice of an ancient notion of righteous conquest, or *digvijaya*, was departed from by the earliest kings only in the northern portions of the Tamil plain following the defeat of the Yadavarayas of Chandragiri.

There, in northern Coromandel, three new provinces, or rajyas, of the Vijayanagara kingdom were created and placed under men loyal to the Sangama rayas. Among these commanders was Manugudeva who governed the new Chandragiri rajya; his great-grandson, Saluva Narasimha, used this as a base, first, to launch his career as a Vijaya-nagara generalissimo and then to win the throne in 1485. The two other new rajyas created from the conquered territory of the Yadava-rayas were Padaividu (modern North Arcot) and Tiruvadi (in modern South Arcot). From here, Vijayanagara commanders main-tained a fortified military presence on the fringes of the prosperous plains of Chingleput and Cuddalore without any apparent inter-ference beyond collecting customs along the main trade routes nearby. For the rest of Tamil country after the first Vijayanagara conquest, old authorities continued until they were swept away by Saluva Narasimha and the Tuluva kings who succeeded him.

OLD CHALLENGES, NEW RESPONSES

The Tuluvas, or more especially Krishnadevaraya, faced a threat to the kingdom as grave as any before. To the north-west of the heartland of the kingdom was the new sultanate at Bijapur with ambitions to seize Raichur; on the north-eastern frontier were the expansionist Gajapatis of Orissa, and to the south were a set of Karnatak chiefs who had opposed the Tuluva usurpation and under the Ummattur family were expanding across the peninsula into Telugu country thus threatening to cut the rayas off from their Tamil dominions.

Krishnadevaraya's solution to these threats was the old and reliable one of a brilliant series of military campaigns followed by a bold policy for reducing chiefly power. In a double-sided attack, chiefs in the core of the kingdom were constrained from above by a system of royal fortresses under Brahman commanders (*durga dandanayaka*) and garrisoned by troops drawn from two sources: Portuguese and Muslim mercenary gunners and footsoldiers recruited from non-peasant, or forest, people (*vedar*) found over much of the central peninsula. From below, the king devised another sort of challenge; this was the enfranchisement of a new strata of lesser chiefs totally dependent upon military service under Krishnadevaraya; these were the 'Poligars' as the British called them (from the Marathi *palegar*, as borrowed from the Tamil *palaiyakka-rar*, and rendered in Telugu as *palegadu* and in Kannada as *palaga-raru*). Literary and inscriptional evidence of the sixteenth century speaks of Krishnadevaraya's Brahman scribal and military officials and his foreign mercenaries, but it is principally to the later documentaion of Colin Mackenzie that we owe our knowledge of the numerous poligar families in the Karnatak-Andhra core of the kingdom who came into existence as military servants of Krishnade-varaya as adjunct infantry and keepers of his forts. His unrivalled power in Vijayanagara history resulted as much from his control of great warrior households in his domain and his reliance on Brahman agents who had no territorial bases of their own as to any other cause.

The brilliance of this strategy for attaining a more centralised state by checking the authority of ancient territorial chiefs was as great as his military achievments. But to appreciate the difficulty of his task and also to anticipate why it failed in the time of his successors, it is necessary to understand the importance of fundamental political and economic division of the peninsular polity he was attempting to fuse. Essentially, his strategy depended on the wealth from areas of high agriculture, population and commerce providing the means for controlling the powerful chieftaincies of the dry upland, the very heart of his kingdom. During the late fifteenth century there were really two countrysides, wholly different rural structures, that conditioned all of the politics of the later Vijayanagara kingdom. However different, though, both kinds of rural structures posed difficulties to a Vijayanagara state striving for the level of centralised power and authority required to fend off other conquest regimes of the time.

POLITICAL GEOGRAPHY

Demography and the moving agricultural frontier are two factors that determined the dual character of political and agrarian institutions in the South. The population of the peninsula south of the Krishna was large relative to other world societies of the sixteenth century. It may have been around 25 million, if the population of all of India was about the 150 million that has been estimated. But then as now, the absolute population of the southern peninsula was less significant than its distribution, bearing in mind the differing capacities of various parts of the peninsula to support people.

The extended Cormandel plain between the deltas of the Krishna-Godavari and Kaveri Rivers and the narrower, but even better watered, plain on the western coast were zones of high populations. Along with these coastal plains, there were other zones of high agriculture and population in the riverine basins of the Palar, Vaigai and Tambraparni and in the Karnatak *maidan* of the upper Kaveri. The whole of the plateau upland between the two coastal plains was, and remains, a zone of thin population, but one that appears to have grown steadily from 1500 as a result of colonisation and natural increase. Present knowledge about these processes at that time permits speculation only, and it should be noted that even after three centuries, that is in 1800, colonisation and natural increase resulted in quite low densities of population in many parts of the upland, about seventy per square mile.

The dry upland of the peninsula ranges between 1,000 and 2,000 feet above the coastal plains from whence came most of the people who colonised the interior. This was a process that was perhaps a thousand years old in 1500, judging from early Tamil poetry which deployed an elaborate poetic code for different landscapes and kinds of production in diverse peninsular environments. Later, in Chola and Pandya times, field agriculturists from both coasts made their way onto the interior upland. Though they were permanent settlers, they nevertheless retained names that recalled their earlier coastal homes. During the same time, organised groups of northern Tamil cultivators set up strong chieftaincies from Nellore across the peninsula to the Karnataka *maidan* and the western ghats. Later, during the period of Hoysala ascendency in the thirteenth century, Kannada-speaking cultivators spread southward in the wake of their kings, as the Hoysala historian J. D. M. Derrett deploringly observed. Derrett spoke of this thirteenth-century expansion southward into the heart of Tamil country as an 'historical aberration' of Ballala II in that it diverted the Hoysalas from their proper mission of creating a 'national empire' in Karnataka. Apart from the anachronistic hyperbole of this judgement, it fails to appreciate the lure of the rich lower Kaveri for the poorly resourced but militarily strong Hoysalas. High agriculture had by then become a prize for the strong of the peninsular dry zone.

More striking even than the Hoysala bid for overlordship in the lower Kaveri was the penetration of Telugus into both the open country of the central Deccan and into Tamil country during the fifteenth century. Telugu cultivating groups had begun migrating from their coastal homelands to the interior upland of Telangana from about the twelfth century and from there they continued their movement westward into what became the heart of the Vijayanagara kingdom. They had modified an irrigation technology based on wells in the coastal and deltaic area to that of rain-fed tanks that the topography of the upland permitted; they also carried a martial tradition that was required to win new tracts from often fierce forest peoples above the ghat, whom they partly displaced and partly incorporated. During the fifteenth century, these hardy warrior-

45

farmers spread from both the coastal regions of their origins and from their new upland villages; they followed the spine of the peninsula southward to the very southern tip of the sub-continent, partly in the service of Telugu conquerers of Tamil country and partly as a continuation of a colonisation process that predated conquest.

Telugu migrations resulted in significant demographic changes in many parts of Tamil country. Referred to as *vadugan* (northerners) by Tamils, Telugu farmers and traders took over parts of the upland stretching southward into Tirunelveli. At times this meant displacing or subordinating older Tamil peasant occupants, but often it meant opening whole new tracts to field cultivation and developing tracts of tank-irrigated agriculture. Both provided the means for supporting numerous small chieftaincies. The latter allied themselves to Telugu commanders of Vijayanagara armies that conquered and reconquered parts of Tamil country during the fifteenth and sixteenth centuries.

The causes of this explosion of Telugu cultivators are disputed. One seems to have been the opportunity to use their fighting skills to augment the wealth that could be produced by dry-land cultivation, which always involved considerable spatial mobility in any case. Another probable cause was the lure of sparsely populated and weakly held tracts of black soils which Telugu cultivators had learned to exploit earlier on the eastern plateau. Telugu settlement in Tamil country follows the distribution of black soils there quite closely as a result of which Telugu farmers and merchants came to constitute major elements of the populations of Coimbatore, Salem, Madurai, and Tirunelveli. To these 'pull' factors a 'push' factor must be added. That is the Muslim pressure for revenue and military manpower as the Bahmani sultans penetrated Telugu districts followed by their successors, the Golconda sultans. Accounts of Telugu migrants in Tamil country given to the British orientalist-official Mackenzie around 1800 refer, quite plausibly, to being driven from their Andhra homelands by the demands of sultan officials. The accounts of many other local Telugu chiefs who remained in Andhra suggest that they took service under the same sultanate regimes that drove compatriots into Tamil country.

Martial peasantries such as these on the agricultural frontiers were not likely to be compliant before the centralising, revenue-seeking regime of the sort that Krishnadevaraya sought to create. The viability of such migrant communities, like that of the Vijayanagara expansion itself, was the same tough, Telugu soldiery. Raising a regular revenue from such cultivators led by fighting chiefs would have been difficult. Less so was gaining revenues from the older, much richer, wet cultivation zones of the peninsula.

Here, the pattern of exploitation by sixteenth-century conquerors seemed to be a combination of tax-farming and tribute methods. Collections at points of production and exchange were contracted out by landed magnates from whom tribute might be demanded by even greater lords, including the Vijayanagara kings themselves. Money was the vital link in all of this, and the increase of money-use is verified in two principal ways. One was the shift in temple endowments during the Vijayanagara age from payments in kind to direct money endowments or to the grant of lands yielding a money income to religious beneficiaries; the other was the vastly increased demand for money taxes of all sorts.

THE APOGEE OF VIJAYANAGARA POWER

That more of land revenue was collected in money during Vijayanagara times than previously is acknowledged by all scholars. One cause for, or consequence of, this greater monetisation is given by Nuniz, a witness to events in the 1530s. Nuniz was describing the system of great commanderies established by Krishnadevaraya for controlling the major chiefs of his realm. This was the moment in the history of the kingdom when central authority was greatest, shortly after Krishnadevaraya's death.

Nuniz listed the leading Vijayanagara 'captains' of Achyutadeva-raya's time, the territories they held, and the money they collected and shared with the king. Nuniz made clear that he was not describing 'officers of the King', but rather 'lords, of the kingdom's greatest territories'. Sewell underscored Nuniz's distinction between 'the King's own personal lands' – 'his home farm so to speak' – and those 'provinces and estates . . . entrusted to a noble who farmed the revenue to his own advantage, paying a fixed sum every year to the king'. This understanding of Nuniz is superior to that of many later scholars who distorted Nuniz's report by reframing it either as a form of bureaucratic or feudal appropriation of rural surpluses.

An instance of the autonomous authority of these great lords of the kingdom comes from an inscription from Mangalagiri, in modern Guntur district, Andhra, referring to Krishnadevaraya's Brahman minister, Saluva Timma, and the latter's two nephews; all held nearly independent authority under the king and were instrumental in the victory gained against Gajapati forces at Kondavidu as can be judged from this inscription ordered by Saluva Timma in 1515, which read in part as follows:

> The great chancellor, the glorious Salva-Timma, the best of ministers, rules the empire of the glorious king Krishnaraya ... When Salva ['hawk'], surnamed Timma ... after having captured the swan-like kings appointed by Gajapati in Kondaviti, is planning an attack, the hostile princes absconding ... resembling birds ... The sister's sons of the glorious minister, Salva Timma, who continued his family, were the excellent ministers Nadinla-Appa and Gopa ... [the former] obtained from the glorious king, Krishna and the minister Timma, a palanquin, two *chauris* [fly wisk emblem of royalty] and a parasol, and the posts of superintendent of [the fortresses at] Vinakonda, Gutti ... of commander in chief of a large army ... and sole governor of that kingdom [Gutti]. The glorious Salva-Timma ... gave to ... Gopa, the best among governors and an excellent minister, the post of governor of Kondaviti, together with an army ... of elephants, horses and infantry and a palanquin and two *chauris*.[4]

First among the 'great captains' whom Nuniz later named was another commander, 'Salvanayque' (Saluva Narasingha Nayaka, or Chellappa), a Tamil Brahman. He was one of those to whom Krishnadevaraya delegated vast governing responsibility, and he retained these powers as Achyutadevaraya's 'minister' and the latter's strong supporter against his rival for the throne in 1529, Aliya Rama Raja. Saluva Nayaka's yearly income was reckoned at over a million gold pieces collected from Tamil chiefs of which he paid a third to Achyutadevaraya and retained the balance in order to maintain his army of 30,000 infantry, 3,000 cavalry, and 30 war

[4] V. R. Ramachandra Dikshitar, ed., *Selected Telugu Inscriptions* (Madras: University of Madras, 1952);Telugu edn., N.Venkata Rao, pp. 128–46.

elephants. His territory comprised most of the Tamil plain. Second after Saluva Nayaka was one whom historians identify as Saluva Timmarasu, a Telugu (Niyogi) Brahman and, like Chellappa, a former minister of Krishnadevaraya. He ruled Telangana for Achyutadevaraya, and his collections were valued at 800,000 gold coins each year. Of this, less than half was reportedly given to the king, and the balance was spent on his army of 25,000 horsemen, 1,500 infantry, and 40 elephants. In addition, Saluva Timmarasu was responsible for three strategic fortresses – Udayagiri, Kondavidu, and Gandikota – as well as for securing two major trade routes linking Coromandel and Andhra coastal areas with Vijayanagara, one through Kondavidu and the other through Penukonda. Other 'captains' in a descending order of gross collections and military obligations held the following territories: Bankapur, a major pepper-producing and cattle-breeding area in north-western Karnataka; the southern border area of the city in central Karnataka; the area around modern Mysore and Bangalore, and others around Chitaldrug, Bangalore, and Kolar. Two other magnates mentioned by Nuniz held the country around the fortress at Gooty, with its valuable diamond mines, and around Mudkal in Raichur. Apart from Saluva Narasimha's domination of Tamil territory, these lordships of the 1530s were either gateways to major commercial zones of the peninsula or tracts commanding trade routes, or they were territories which had strategic importance in the defence of the Vijayanagara core area of the Tungabhadra-Krishna basin.

RESOURCE LIMITS OF VIJAYANAGARA KINGS

Even the most powerful Vijayanagara rulers of the sixteenth century – Krishnadevaraya, Achyutadevaraya, and Rama Raja – enjoyed only a part of the revenues collected from the richest provinces of the realm. These, of course, all lay well outside the kingdom's core. One was the Karnataka *maidan* of the upper Kaveri, but it was gradually lost to any substantial appropriative benefit by Vijayanagara kings during Achyutadevaraya's time when a young chief, *odeya* (which becomes the dynastic name 'Wodeyar'), established his family's control over the fortress of Srirangapattanam. This family seems to have come to the region of the upper Kaveri, around Halebid, following the demise of the Hoysalas whom they served. Having entered the service of Vijayanagara, they benefited from Krishnadevaraya's defeat of the Ummattur chiefs of around Srirangapattanam, increasing their lordship over the fertile lands around Mysore and Bangalore. Tribute and soldiers were supplied by the growing chiefdom during the times of Saluva Narasimha and Krishnadevaraya, but after that the Wodeyar chiefs slipped central obligations and ruled with increasing independence.

Another rich zone of agriculture far from the capital were the wealthy, surplus-producing regions of Tamil country: the Palar basin in the centre and the Kaveri basin in the South. These were under the stewardship of Saluva Narasimha Nayaka from 1510 to 1531. This Tamil Brahman enjoyed great titles, responsibilities, and privileges during the time of Krishnadevaraya. He even made land grants to temples without referring to the king. Chellappa, as he was called, must also have passed a substantial tribute to Krishnadevaraya as he did for a few years to Achyutadevaraya, but this financial support to the latter was not nearly as important as Chellappa's military support of Achyutadevaraya against the conspiracy of Rama Raja.

Chellappa rose against Achyutadevaraya in concert with other Tamil chiefs in 1531. Inscriptional evidence of the time suggests that the reason for Chellappa's rebellion was his resentment that Achyutadevaraya interfered with his powers to make and protect religious endowments in Chola country. Most historians reject this as an implausible cause, but serious political consequences could well have resulted from challenging so significant an aspect of regal power as Chellappa had long possessed, even under Krishnadevaraya. Other reasons for Chellappa's rebellion pertain to the conspiracies of Aliya Rama Raja. The latter's plans to displace Achyutadevaraya began with the removal of such stalwart supporters as Chellappa and their replacement in the rich provinces they controlled by his own supporters. However, when Chellappa was defeated in 1532, he was succeeded by Salakaraju, an affinal kinsman of Achyutadevaraya and the latter's keen supporter against Rama Raja; he ruled rule over Tamil country until 1543 when his royal ambitions were revealed in a rebellion against central authority.

1 Elephant stables

2 Courtyard of the Virupaksha temple

3 Octagonal fountain

4 Large step-well

5 A view of the towered gateway (*gopuram*) of the Virupaksha temple

6 Eastern towered gateway of the Virupaksha temple

7 Scenes from the Krishna legend in the Hazara Rama temple

8 The Pattabhirama temple seen through the Chinna Hudiam temple

Thus, the Kaveri milch-cow of resources for a central Vijayanagara exchequer proved difficult to milk. During the time of
Krishnadevaraya and a few years of his successor, most of the
Tamil plain was under Chellappa who proved a loyal servant and
provided some financial assistance to Krishnadevaraya and his
successor as well as a great deal of political support. For the next
ten or so years, after Chellappa was defeated, the vast wealth of
the Tamil plain and its ports was in the hands of the ambitious
and powerful Salakaraju family and provided them with the means
to pursue dynastic aspirations of their own. Moreover, the wealth
available from other parts of the far south of Tamil country
remained out of even the merely potential tributary catchment of
Vijayanagara kings. Chellappa's allies in revolt included two chieftains who held most of Madurai and Tirunelveli; another was the
raja of Travancore. By their alliance with Chellappa, they not only
denied the Vijayanagara kings of the resources and homage of
much of Tamil country, but required an expensive campaign to
thwart.

If regular revenue from the richest areas of South India proved as
difficult for the rulers of the kingdom to command as that from the
numerous, tough chieftains of the dry upland of the realm, what
then of possibly large revenues from the vigorous international trade
around the coasts of the peninsula? There is some evidence to
support that this first became available in the time of Saluva
Narasimha, while he served Vijayanagara and, later, when he was
king late in the century.

But when this evidence is carefully evaluated, it is difficult to
sustain the view that a major and regular component of the revenues
of the Kingdom came from the great and growing trade at Arabian
Sea ports. Accounts of foreigners – Europeans and Muslims –
confirm that Vijayanagara rulers like Saluva Narasimha and the.
Tuluva kings offered importers high prices for horses, even dead
ones, so as to monopolise the traffic in horses. However, there is
almost no information about foreign trade that can be gleaned from
indigenous historical sources of the Vijayanagara period, notwithstanding the considerable, ostensible importance attributed to
foreign trade by Krishnadevaraya. This is found in the Telugu
didactic poem, *Amuktamalyada*, thought either to have been com-

posed by the king or purveying his ideas. In the fourth canto of the work, Krishnadevaraya maximises as follows:

> A king should improve the harbours of his country and so encourage its commerce that horses, elephants, precious gems, sandalwood, pearls and other articles are freely imported ... He should arrange that the foreign sailors who land in his country on account of storms, illness and exhaustion are looked after in a manner suitable to their nationalities ... Make the merchants of distant foreign countries who import elephants and good horses be attached to yourself by providing them with daily audience, presents and allowing decent profits. Then those articles will never go to your enemies.[5]

If the Vijayanagara kings realised even a fraction of the great wealth generated by trade along their western coast, this might have sustained the military and other works necessary to achieve Krishnadevaraya's quest for a centralised kingship. Extant indigenous evidence indicates that the most important centres of foreign trade could have yielded little on a regular basis to the central treasury of the kingdom.

Tulu country was one of the chief areas of this international trade and was probably the ancestral homeland of kings of the third dynasty. Along this Arabian Sea littoral were several of the major emporia of the time: Bhatakal, as already mentioned Barakuru, and Mangaluru. The monograph on Kanara by K. V. Ramesh exhaustively examines the extant epigraphical evidence and shows that references to the international trade that we know existed were both rare and indirect. While he notes that most taxes were paid in money, as elsewhere in the kingdom, and that each of the two headquarters of the province – Barakuru and Mangaluru – had mints whose coinage circulated there along with coins from elsewhere, Ramesh insists that most revenue collected was from agricultural production. He notes few references to commercial taxes as compared to the many pertaining to agricultural production.

Still, Ramesh has much to say about corporate mercantile and artisanal bodies throughout Kanara or Tuluva. The wealth and prestige of such groups are celebrated in their donative inscriptions on Hindu and Jaina shrines, where they figure as arbitrators in

[5] Rangasvami Sarasvati, 'Political Maxims of the Emperor-Poet Krishnadeva Raya', *The Journal of Indian History* part 3 (1925) pp. 70 and 72

temple disputes and as protectors of religious establishments of all kinds. There are also references to all kinds of internationally traded commodities handled by merchants of Tuluva including imported ceramic and cloth wares from China and export goods brought into Tulu country from the peninsula above the western ghats. The wealth derived from this trade is attested by Portuguese and Muslim commentators of the time.

Impediments to centralised appropriation of some part of that wealth were numerous. The rule of Vijayanagara kings or their agents (*karyakarta*) was intermittent and often weak from the time that Tulu country was made a royal province by Devaraya II. The coastal tract had to be reconquered by Devaraya, but this made little difference, and Kanara was conquered yet again in 1522 during the reign of Krishnadevaraya. The latter led an army there against one of the several large, ancient chiefs of the region, and though the king remained for sometime while a commander of his fought the Portuguese, he left behind no permanent apparatus for revenue extraction. Indeed, between his time and that of Sadasivaraya, that is from 1529 to 1576, none of the governors who ruled from Barakuru or Mangaluru were appointed by Vijayanagara kings.

Evidence of Kanara indicates that Vijayanagara kings can have received little on a regular basis from its valuable trade. That was the preserve of a set of Hindu and Jaina magnates whose local authority was fortified by an interlinking of several distinctive elements, which proved as difficult for Vijayanagara kings to penetrate as it was to prove for the British in the nineteenth century. One was that landholding in this highly favoured zone of wet cultivation was based on compact 'estates', as the British were to call them, under the control of warrior families who were linked to ruling chiefs (often calling themselves rajas) through kinship and marriage. Grain and pepper production of the region was in the hands of trading corporations, called *nagara* and *settikara*, who paid a part of the profits of this trade to these local magnates. The difference between the two trade corporations seemed to be that the first was probably involved in international trade and the second in domestically produced commodities and grains. In addition, there were in Tulu country corporate groups of artisans, called *hanjamana* or *nagara-hanjamana*, distinguishing, again, producers and traders of locally produced commodities for local exchange from those involved in overseas trade. These corporations were highly localised and some of the leading centres of trade, such as Barakuru, had three local *settikara* groups. Endowments to Hindu and Jaina shrines indicate that such groups operated within discrete chiefly territories except in the main foreign trade centres; all traders enjoyed the protection of chiefs in whose territories they operated and to whom they paid revenue on their trade and industrial production. It is probable that Kanara magnates of the time participated in the trade through agents called *rajasresthi*, royal merchants, as other west-coast rulers did during the twelfth century and later.

Opportunities for central appropriation of wealth from overseas trade on the opposite, or Coromandel, coast appear no more promising as the historical relations of Vijayanagara there make clear.

COROMANDEL POLITICS

Early in the first dynasty, two powerful chiefdoms on the eastern frontier of Vijayanagara were conquered. This was to gain security against Reddi and Velama kingdoms of coastal Andhra and Telangana, but another reason was to open the rich trade coasts and adjacent zones of advanced agriculture to Vijayanagara domination and its tributary catchment.

The first of these conquered tracts was centred on the northern Tamil plain around Chandragiri where the Yadavaraya chiefs had held sway; the second was in the area south of that, including much of the modern Arcots then under the Sambuvaraya chiefs. The Yadavarayas were local, but claimed to be connected with the ancient Eastern Chalukyas and Cholas; the Sambuvarayas were Vanniyar chiefs, part of that group of peasant warriors – like the Reddis and Velamas of Andhra – who rose to local prominence under the imperial Cholas to become the dominant peasantry in many parts of the Arcots and Kanchipuram by the fourteenth century. Both of these chiefdoms were defeated by Vijayanagara soldiers under the command of the general Mangudeva, a subordinate of Kumara Kampana, brother of the king Harihara II, with whom Mangu campaigned in southern Tamil country. His reward

for these services was the governorship of Chandragiri, newly constituted from part of the territory taken from the Yadavarayas.
Mangudeva and his descendants extended the Chandragiri rajya
northward to include Guntur and neighbouring parts of southern
Andhra; they also gained territory to the south as a result of Vijayanagara forays into Tamil country in the time of Devaraya II, into whose
family the Chandragiri chiefs were now married. These successors to
Mangu now called themselves, with some justice, 'Saluva' ('hawk'),
and the greatest of them was Saluva Narasimha whose rise from
around 1460 culminated with the throne itself in 1485.

Saluva Narasimha drove the Orissan Gajapati from the border
country between Karnataka and Andhra and pursued them northward over 150 miles to fortified Udayagiri, which he seized.
Returning south, he established direct Vijayanagara authority over
the entire Tamil plain for the first time, reaching Ramesvaram in the
1470s. Like other generalissimos of the fifteenth century – Perma-
ladeva, Devaraya II's commander and possibly his co-ruler, and
Mangudeva, his own ancestor – Narasimha commanded a large
royal army for service against Muslim and Hindu enemies; and like
the others, the army was Narasimha's instrument for gaining ever
greater power within the kingdom. Even before he seized the throne
for himself, military subordinates of his had begun to make names
for themselves. One was Isvara Nayaka, whose son Narasa Nayaka
established the Tuluva Dynasty in 1491; the other was Aravidi
Bukka, whose descendants established the last Vijayanagara dynasty
in the 1540s.

From the very onset of the loose Vijayanagara overlordship in the
fourteenth century, most of the Coromandel plain was under rulers
who were independent of royal control. The Coromandel's trade
emporia from Motupalli in the delta of the Krishna-Godavari to
Tuticorin in the far south and its high agriculture from Chandragiri
to the Tambraparni basin in Tirunelveli yielded wealth to other
lords. At first, these included the subjugated Sambuvarayas, Cholas,
and Pandyas, but in the time of Krishnadevaraya, the beneficiaries
had come to include a set of politico-military personages who
sprung from the Vijayanagara armies. The latter, soon after the
reconquest of Tamil country, launched themselves upon independent careers which ultimately limited royal appropriations from the

wealth agriculture and trade of Coromandel and then threatened the very overlordship of the kingdom on that coastal plain.

KRISHNADEVARAYA'S KINGDOM
AND ITS DISSOLUTION

But before opposition in Tamil country could be quelled, Krishnadevaraya faced more immediate dangers on taking the throne vacated by his half-brother, Vira Narasimha, in 1509.

Danger was removed by a series of brilliant military campaigns against Muslims and Gajapatis on the northern and eastern flanks of the Vijayanagara core territory, and Krishnadevaraya returned to his troublesome Tamil subjects with enhanced reputation and confidence. His achievements were posted a mere six months after his coronation in an inscription engraved on the Virupaksha temple in Hampi. In this record of January 1510, the titles of 'Hindu Sultan' and 'fever to the elephants of Gajapati' were added to his coronation title of being an incarnation of the god Krishna. Next, the king turned to a quarter from which a threat was posed on his western flank by a Karnatak chief of the Ummattur family. Gangaraja had built strong fortresses in the upper Kaveri at Srirangapattanam and Sivasamudram; from these fastnesses he had launched campaigns across the Karnataka and Andhra plains to Penukonda, threatening both western and southern approaches to Vijayanagara. To subdue Gangaraja, Krishnadevaraya is said to have summoned a large force of cavalry and infantry from local military chiefs who were as worried as the king by the expansion of Gangaraja's authority, and the latter was killed in 1512 and his fortress at Sivasamudram razed. Notwithstanding this rebellion, as it was conceived, Gangaraja's son and descendants were permitted to continue to rule from Srirangapattanam. Later, southern Karnataka was to fall under the rule of three of those military leaders who had joined in Krishnadevaraya's campaign against Gangaraja of whom one, Kempe Gauda, became the ruler of Bangalore and its countryside and another, the Tamil Brahman generalissimo Saluva Govindaraja, was entrusted to the government of parts of southern Karnataka.

Other of Krishnadevaraya's trusted soldiers of these several campaigns were also destined for important independent careers.

Two of these were Nagama Nayaka and Chellappa Saluva Nayaka, brother of Saluva Govindaraja. Krishnadevaraya gave both major responsibilities and privileges in Tamil country, and both were ultimately to rise against their Vijayanagara masters, Nagama against Krishnadevaraya and Chellappa against Achyutadevaraya. The territories from which the rebellions of both were launched had been formed by lands taken from the ancient holders of royal authority in Tamil country and placed under Vijayanagara men who, in the end, violated their sovereigns' trusts, but were true to the times in seeking royal fortunes for themselves.

Nagama Nayaka's treachery is recounted in chronicles of the rise of the nayaka kingdom of Madurai. The generalissimo Nagama was supposedly dispatched by Krishnadevaraya to punish the Virasekhara Chola for despoiling the Pandayans who were under protection of Vijayanagara. Having dealt with the Chola, Nagama proclaimed Madurai his own. He, in turn, was denied the fruits of disloyalty by his son, Visvanatha Nayaka, who delivered his father over to Krishnadevaraya. As a reward, the more loyal subject than son, Visvanatha, was appointed governor of a large part of southern Tamil country; he and his son Krishnappa supported successive rayas until the sack of the city in 1565. Then, with the Vijayanagara king in flight, Krishnappa set an independent Madurai kingdom whose expansion and consolidation owed much to the help of his father's able minister, Ariyanatha Mudaliar. Thus, the extensive domains of the ancient Pandyas, valuable alike for its agriculture and its trade coast, provided little regular sustenance to Vijayanagara kings and required several chastising campaigns even to secure homage.

In a like manner, other Vijayanagara generalissimos sent to pacify the Tamil plain and secure Vijayanagara hegemony there ended up by launching independent kingdoms. One was in a territory reaching from Nellore to the Kollidam (Coleroon) River, with a capital at the fortress of Gingee. This was Tubaki Krishnappa, son of Krishnadevaraya's general Vaiyappa Nayaka. The even more valuable domain of the Kaveri basin was also denied to Krishnadevaraya's successors by descendants of the latter's general, Sivappa Nayaka. Unlike the Brahman Chellappa, Sivappa was the descendant of peasant warriors who formed the core of the rayas' armies; for his service, Sivappa became a close companion of Achyutadevaraya and even married into the latter's family before being appointed to Tanjavur. Inscriptions from the Kaveri basin confirm that Sivappa remained loyal, but he seems to have avoided some of the campaigns launched in the far south by Rama Raja of the Arividu family, who was Sadasivaraya's powerful generalissimo and virtual co-ruler. These campaigns of Rama Raja were to regain Vijayanagara control of Chandragiri and to punish a set of Tamil chiefs for failing to pay tribute. Not only did Sivappa stay clear of such military expeditions, but he seems to have devoted himself to enriching Tanjavur beyond its grain surpluses by entering into arrangements with the Portuguese whereby the latter paid generously to have trading stations along the coast of Tanjavur.

In the grandest days of Vijayanagara, during the time of Krishnadevaraya, it is obvious that the resources capable of being regularly appropriated by its kings were those in the Tungabhadra heartland of the kingdom. This was not a small region, nor were its resources meagre. That heartland extended over 30,000 square miles, from the Kannada-speaking, modern Bellary district to the Telugu-speaking districts of Kurnool and Cuddapah. This was approximately the same territory administered by Thomas Munro between 1800 and 1808 as collector of the 'Ceded Districts' of the Madras Presidency, and its population in the sixteenth century may not have been very different from that two centuries later, that is, about two million.

Tuluva kings of the first half of the sixteenth century drew upon a large agricultural zone in the midst of whose dominantly dry cropped fields were small regions of high agriculture based on tank irrigation. In this region there were among the best cotton soils in the peninsula as well as some of the largest pasturages that supported the herding of both cattle and sheep. Thus, cotton and woollen goods were exported from the region as well as bullocks. Bullocks were used in large numbers to move commodities over a peninsular trade region that centred on the city of Vijayanagara; bullocks also began to replace others who had long been aristocrats of the animal kingdom – war horses and elephants – because bullocks pulled the guns that now appeared in all armies.

The north-western flank of this peninsular trade system centred on Vijayanagara was Bankapur and the south-western flank was

Srirangapattanam; both of these Karnatak towns were linked to major emporia along the Arabian Sea coast from Chaul in the north to Cannanore in the south. Substantial customs dues were collected from the trade, these interior towns, and others like Mysore and Ikkeri, also served as assembly points for commodities and therefore additional custom revenues. On the eastern flank of this trade system there were the Coromandel ports from Motupalli south to Pulicat, just north of modern Madras. They were connected to Vijayanagara by a major route linking the important pilgrimage centre at Tirupati, the manufacturing and trade town of Penukonda, and the important fortress towns of Chandragiri and Chitaldrug.

Scattered over this dry upland heart of the kingdom there were many pockets of high cultivation and population based on the development of tank irrigation by chiefs such as Saluva Narasimha. He not only increased irrigation in the Chandragiri area, his base, but also encouraged temple authorities at the nearby temples of Tirupati and Kalahasti to invest money endowments to improve tanks and irrigation canals in hundreds of nearby temple villages. This practice was imitated by other magnates, among the most important of whom were the eighty or so within the Vijayanagara heartland itself.

Contemporary inscriptions and later accounts collected by the first British administrators in the core of the old Vijayanagara kingdom provide valuable evidence on the political authority of these chiefs, most of whom were called 'Poligars' by the British. The heyday of these chiefs was the first half of the sixteenth century, but most seem to have come into existence during the early sixteenth century as a result of Krishnadevaraya's policies for diminishing older chiefly families.

Thomas Munro, the famous first collector of the region, regarded these chiefs as the major centres of resistance to British rule, and he justified their removal on the grounds of their historical political authority. In Munro's time, 2,000 villages were held by eighty poligari families of different statuses. The highest and perhaps oldest of such local magnates are found in modern Bellary district. One was the chief of the Anegondi, calling himself the Tirumala Raja and claiming descent from a Vijayanagara ruling family; this chief held 114 villages in 1800. Fifty miles south-west of Anegondi and Hampi was the Harapanahalli poligar; this family seems to have been established in the sixteenth century by a Lingayat chief, Dadappa Nayar, on the modest basis of his watchman's (*taliyar*) rights in two villages.

The number of villages held by these numerous ruling families in Vijayanagara times is not always known from the family records said to have been consulted by Munro. Those of the Anegondi and Harapanahalli chiefs during the sixteenth century are not known, but another, the Jaramali poligar, held 309 villages then and appears to have supplied a force of 3,000 foot-soldiers and 500 horsemen to the kings. The Rayadrug chief, Venkatapati Nayaka, paid no money to Vijayanagara kings either, but contributed 2,000 infantry. Evidence of around 1800 suggests that other of the eighty poligars of this Vijayanagara heartland held some villages free of any payment to the Vijayanagara kings and held other villages as tax-farmers. In addition, they were obliged to maintain some mounted and some foot-soldiers for royal service. Many of the smaller poligars and most of the infantry they maintained were Bedars or Boyas, swidden cultivators and hunters of the forests, and of these many were Lingayats. During the sixteenth century, also, several of these chiefs were Muslims. Munro estimated that over 1,200 villages were under poligars until 1660 when the former Vijayanagara heartland had come under the control of the Bijapur sultans or their commanders, such as Shahji, father of Sivaji. Of these villages, 682 were held free of any money demands and 535 were held as tax-farms for which money was paid to sultanate officials. The same eighty poligars supplied a total of 29,000 infantry and 1,200 cavalry to Bijapur armies.

As a rough estimate, half of the villages thought to be held by local chiefs in the core of the kingdom paid some money to the Vijayanagara kings. The probability is that much of the surplus production in other villages of the core of the kingdom was shared between the Rayas and Brahmans and other religious beneficiaries so that in the very core of the kingdom, the royal share of surpluses may not have been very high. Elsewhere it was less. The revenue beneficiaries of the thriving international commerce seem to have been the numerous, small lordships on the western coast and the larger lordships on the eastern, or Coromandel, coast. Kings could not have benefited except when a great commander like Chellappa in the time of Krishnadevaraya was loyal. Also, while it is true that revenue from much of agriculture was in cash, as were inland customs and dues extracted from merchants and artisans, there is no evidence that this money – or much of it – found its way to Vijayanagara and the treasury of the kings.

The resources for achieving what Krishnadevaraya sought to curb the territorial magnates of the peninsula were therefore not abundant. His wars brought prizes to the city and paid for its many monuments, but it is doubtful, again, that this contributed more to central power than was lost by the spread of military leaders ever more deeply into the peninsular countryside. Warfare tested and fortified the military capabilities of the numerous military chiefs of the south; wars also spread the poligar institution. Fighters seized or were granted income from villages as a means of maintaining the petty armed forces used in the wars of greater lords; otherwise, local cultivating and trading groups seeking some protection from the violence of the times paid for the protection of poligars in many places of the far south, as implied by the term *padikaval* used in Ramnad and Pudukkottai. No chieftains could remain aloof from nearby warfare, which was bound to lead to a reshuffling of local power that left the strong stronger and pushed the weaker into yet greater vulnerability and submission. Scattered contests for local dominance changed balances between local lordships and the communal bases of their rule on the one hand and between these local lords and the kings of Vijayanagara or their agents on the other.

THE OLD AND NEW POLITICAL ORDER

The sixteenth-century system of political relations marks a major change from all states before Vijayanagara in the South; it is also different from the first century of Vijayanagara kings.

Previous kingdoms – Cholas, Pandyas, Hoysalas, and Kakatiyas – were aggregates of numerous chieftaincies over localised, communal organisation. The *nadu* in many parts of the South, the *okkalu* of Karnataka, and the highly territorialised caste organisation of Reddis and other dominant agricultural communities all point to this underlying character of pre- and early-Vijayanagara society and polity. Kings then differed from other lords in having immediate mastery over areas of high agriculture and population, in being conquerors, and in being anointed. The authority of many pre-Vijayanagara kings and all chiefs was an extension of communal morality and lineage or clan organisation. Most chiefs in late medieval times, at any rate, sought to escape the confines of the communal sources of their authority by establishing relations with anointed kings, and seeking thereby to acquire some extra-communal, royal authority over resources and people; the kings with whom such relations came to exist magnified their royal claims thereby, but the substance of their authority was command over the rich and populous river valleys during pre-Vijayanagara times.

Then, too, kings claimed rights to a major share of material and human resources within their realms as *ksattra*, possession by lordship. Chola kings, for example, enjoyed this in the Kaveri basin – the core of their realm – and less consistently in the Palar basin as well; they claimed the same lordly possession in Pandya country, but never achieved a sustained mastery there. Non-royal, or chiefly, power and authority arose from headship over dominant, local peasant groups. Yet, titles affected by chiefs among Tamils, Telugus, and Kannadiyans all derive from a Dravidian root, *utai*, which, as *utaimai*, had the same meaning as *ksattra*. Hence, the language of royal and chiefly claims was the same, and this is one manifestation of what I elsewhere call the 'segmentary state'. According to this notion, the Chola state and other medieval states of the South existed as states in the recognition by dispersed locally based lordships of the ritual sovereignty of the most powerful of their number, the anointed king. Relations between such autochthons and anointed kings during the pre-Vijayanagara age were essentially ritual, expressed in the dharmic idioms of royal protection and lordly service. This occurs in the Tamil *muvendavelar* (a chief who serves the three anointed kings over Tamils: Chola, Pandya, or Chera) adopted by great men of the Chola age.

During the time of Krishnadevaraya, as well as before and after, sovereignty in the Vijayanagara kingdom was conceived of as divided or shared. Its kings claimed to rule the whole of the peninsula south of the Krishna River, a claim which is denominated here as ritual sovereignty, distinguishing, thereby, between the political authority that numerous ruling families enjoyed as possessors of *ksattra* or *utai*, everywhere in the kingdom, and the recognition by all of these *utaiyar* of the special status of the king. The latter, by virtue of his anointment and his responsibility for the protection and welfare of all in the kingdom, possessed powers conferred by *rajadharma* as well as *ksattra* in his central domain. These two sources of authority – *ksattra/utai* and *rajadharma* – were complementary; together they fulfilled the conception of appropriate authority in Hindu kingdoms of the age, including Vijayanagara. It is in this sense that the concept of *dayada*, or shared sovereignty, is crucial, and it is also in this sense that the Vijayanagara state, and others of the age, may be regarded as polities of chiefs.

Monarchies of the medieval age in South India were intended to express and preserve chiefly authority and were therefore founded on a class formation in which the ruling class was a stratum of chiefs. The legitimacy of the latter stemmed from their protection of a whole structure of communal entitlements of stratified groups within their chiefdoms. Among the latter were the leading landholding groups, major merchant and artisanal groups and most religious bodies. Ultimately, the success of Krishnadevaraya's policy of reducing the authority of chiefs and increasing royal authority depended on the conviction of many in his kingdom that their collective entitlements would be preserved under the greater centralisation he sought. To the extent that his measures increased and strengthened prebendal entitlements, or new rights to wealth, the king's measures must have seemed as threatening to communally-organised constituents of chiefly authority as to the ancient and new stratum of chiefs themselves.

Krishnadevaraya's bold attempt to extend the reach of central authority was a major innovation of the age, though it was based on certain prior developments. Before his time, the ubiquitous Vijayanagara term for the bond between lesser lord and king was *karyakarta*, that is 'agent', a seeming denial of any autochthonous authority by the king's chiefly subjects. Those with the title of 'nayaka' in Vijayanagara times represented a new kind of local lordship in two ways. One was the rhetorical shift from the earlier implication of terms like *nattar*, the leaders of the *nadu*, which signified some tract of land and its dominant cultivators – the ancient sense of *janapada*. During Vijayanagara times, such a conception continues, but must then be understood not as absolute dominion – arising from a group having tamed a forest to regular cultivation or from a conquest of existing cultivators, about which all south Indians would have agreed earlier. Now, there was little of such claims of absolute dominion, but only relative communal conceptions or rights to be set off against new and different rights of agency held by powerful individuals. A second difference was that rights of agency were derived from a king, hence these are prebendal rights, different from and in potential conflict with rights derived from a community or communal rights.

The meaning of lordship began to be transformed during the time of Devaraya II with the granting of enlarged importance to soldiers and to military rank and associated political powers and superior landed rights based on military service to the rayas. This is the meaning of the term *amara* (from the Sankrit *samara*, 'war') and the associated specific entitling land right, *amara-magani*, and the title, *amara-nayaka*. Lordship thus becomes a conception of authority that, in being understood as derived from the distant authority of a high Vijayanagara official, say a *mahapradhani*, or the king, challenged and weakened locally-derived and protected communal rights, even when the agent was not actually a 'foreigner', as the Telugu *vadugan* was in Tamil country.

Though there are differences among historians of Tamil country, Karnataka, and Andhra about the decline of local corporate institutions and communal rights during the Vijayanagara age, on the whole it seems true that rights to local resources and power changed during the sixteenth century. This was the general effect of the confrontation of older systems of communal rights by new prebendal claims of all sorts. New and challenging claims are observed in another aspect of lordship in South India. That is, the fiscal demands of all superordinate authorities were satisfied only by money. During Chola times, references to taxes in money (*kasu ayam*) are rare in comparison to payments in kind or in labour. By the sixteenth century, ten categories of money taxes (*suvarna sunka*) were collected that had scarcely ever been mentioned before. These included money taxes on agricultural and herding, on forest products; on various industrial and commercial activities, including taxes on goods imported from overseas; military and police taxes, or fees, paid for the protection afforded by a local fort, military commander, or to a local watchman, called *kavalgar* or *taliyar*; professional taxes paid not only by barbers, washermen, and goldsmiths, but also by leatherworkers (*madiga*), hunters (*bedar* or *boya*) and even by Brahman priests; sets of communal taxes (*samaya-sunka*), including marriage taxes and fines levied on specific castes such as one of the time of Venkataraya II (reign 1586–1614) raised for the benefit of a Reddi headman (*desai*, from *desa* or 'locality'). Notwithstanding all of these, and other money taxes found in sixteenth-century inscriptions, neither Venkataramanayya, who most completely canvassed these terms, nor other scholars of the period have been able to determine whether such money taxes went to a central treasury. Prebendal entitlements, such as *amara nayankara*, that came into existence during the later fifteenth century were not the cause of the monetisation of the age, but without that these entitlements could not have been realised by the new stratum of prebendal lords.

Nor can it be said that these new prebendal rights were legislated by Vijayanagara kings. It is well to remember that the records of payments to satisfy the demands of superior political authorities came not from account books of revenue departments, nor even from contemporary administrative texts like the Mughal *Ain-i-Akbari*, but from thousands of records of religious endowments and later texts collected by Mackenzie.

Apart from prebendal rights and institutions, such as *nayankara*, the Vijayanagara age saw temples emerge as major political arenas. Temples and sectarian (*matha*) centres were supported by those in political authority through their donations of money revenues from that income enjoyed as a political right. This was the same whether the grantor was Krishnadevaraya, who gave 10,000 gold coins to various major temples in Tamil country, or a headman for the benefit of a local shrine.

Arjun Appadurai demonstrated how money as well as land was circulated in such a way as to lash together three great institutions of the Vijayanagara age: kings and their great commanders, the heads of major Hindu sectarian groups, and temples. He documents how the first Vijayanagara incursions into Tamil country resulted in close relations between the conquerors and such major temples as that at Srirangam through the intermediary activities of sectarian leaders. The latter – members of the Vaishnava Uttamanambi family – translated gifts from Vijayanagara kings to temple managers at Srirangam in return for which the royal or official donor received the first and highest honours from the god Sriranganatha, thus fortifying the royal claims of the conquerors. The Uttamanambi intermediaries, for their part, assumed a more strategic place in the management of the temple. The same process was repeated in many other places, then and later. Saluva Narasimha seized commanding influence at the important Vishnu temple of Tirupati in collaboration with another sect leader, Kandadai Ramanuja Aiyangar. Narasimha's large endowments of land and money were made to the god Venkatesvara through Kandadai Ramanuja who was thereby entitled to portions of the honours and wealth which was used to advance his own position and that of his followers with authorities of the temple. Appadurai shows how this was replicated elsewhere, including at the Sri Parasarati Swami temple at Triplicane in modern Madras during the time of the Vijayanagara kings Sadasivaraya and Venkata II (1537–1614).

Appadurai's brilliant analysis concluded that kings and other great men of the Vijayanagara age exchanged material resources which they commanded for temple honours through the agency of sect leaders in order to gain control of political constituencies that might otherwise have proved refractory. It is important to notice that there appears to have been no attempt by these Telugu outsiders to preserve an identity as outsiders as might have been thought useful to a conquering élite. The contrary is the case. The objective of these royal agents, notwithstanding the efforts of Vijayanagara kings, especially Krishnadevaraya, was not to forge a unified and centralised polity out of the formidable divisions in the southern peninsula. Rather, the use by Telugu and Kannadiyan outsiders of the temple and sectarian leaders with large, popular followings was to enable ambitious military commanders and chiefs of the time to create political regimes and to establish political relationships that were essentially local, more integrated with older forms of affinity and organisation – thus more manageable, than that achievable under the imperial umbrella of Vijayanagara kings. This was one of the factors that proved the undoing of Krishnadevaraya's centralising innovation, but there were even more general problems.

CRISES OF THE NEW ORDER

Two crises threatened the protection of his imperial umbrella; both arose from the activities of Krishnadevaraya's kinsman, Aliya (which means son-in-law) Rama Raja. In 1529 and again in 1535, he challenged Achyutadevaraya, Krishnadevaraya's chosen successor for the throne of the kingdom, and though these attempts failed, his actions did much to divide the great imperial families of Andhra and set the stage for their internecine warfare shortly after. A second way in which Rama Raja laid the foundations for the demise of the Vijayanagara kingdom was by his aggressive interventions into the territories of the sultanates on the kingdom's northern frontier. His adventures there temporarily converted the warring successors of the Bahmani rulers of the Deccan into a coalition against Vijayanagara which resulted in a humiliating defeat, Rama Raja's death and the sack of the city. The first of these two portentous actions by Rama Raja must be considered here, leaving for a later discussion the conditions which led to the humiliating defeat of 1565.

Historians of the kingdom have condemned Rama Raja for abandoning Krishnadevaraya's centralising initiatives against territorial chiefs of the realm, but they have been more forgiving of his Machiavellian policies against the Deccani sultans, possibly because they have accepted the purportedly dharmic mission of the kingdom. Neither position seems justified. To take up the adventurism in the Deccan first, it should be said that the Raichur and Krishna River frontiers of the kingdom were never accepted by Vijayanagara kings as fixed; these tracts were always prospective areas of expansion for the fighting chiefs of the core area of the kingdom, just as Tamil country was. Rama Raja's interventions in the Deccan differed from others in being more successful and in being carried out by diplomacy as well as military force. As to his reversal of Krishnadevaraya's centralising policies, this was but a return to the established politics of the age, the recognition that the kingdom was in essence a polity of chiefs and a state only in the sense that the numerous and powerful chiefs of the southern peninsula recognised and offered their homage to Vijayanagara kings.

Rama Raja was one of several sons of Aravidi Bukka, a commander of Saluva Narasimha's armies and a soldier who, with the Tuluva Narasa Nayaka, helped to make Narasimha the power behind the last Sangama holders of the throne and then their successor. During the reign of Narasimha, Aravidi Bukka attained the independent status of generalissimo, a position he fortified by shifting his support from Narasimha's successor to Narasa Nayaka and the new Tuluva kings. He was one of the great men of the kingdom present at Krishnadevaraya's coronation in January 1510, and for his support Krishnadevaraya gave one of his daughters and other honours to the generalissimo's capable son, Rama Raja. As an affine of the royal family and heir to the large, well-placed followership of his father, Rama Raja contested for the Vijayanagara throne in 1529. His challenge was formidable because his kinsmen held some of the strongest fortresses in the Vijayanagara heartland: Adoni, Kurnool, Awuku, and Nandyala.

Achyutadevaraya survived this threat by his courage and impressive allies of his own. When his brother died, Achyutadevaraya had himself crowned at the Tirupati and Kalahasti temples, the major Vishnu and Siva shrines of the eastern heartland of the kingdom, near Chandragiri where he had either been content, or constrained by Krishnadevaraya, to live, well away from the capital. His powerful brothers-in-law, the Salakarajus, one of whom had served as the late king's treasurer, threw their support to the king as did Krishnadevaraya's Brahman military commanders. Of the latter, the most important was Chellappa Saluva Nayaka, governor of Chola country. The combination of moral advantage in being his brother's choice, his timely temple coronations, and the strength of his allies seems to have checked Rama Raja's scheme and permitted Achyutadevaraya to proceed to Vijayanagara for a third coronation. He followed this, as his brother had done, with creditable victories, throwing back another Gajapati invasion of Andhra – the last – and checking incursions from the Golkonda sultans on the eastern frontier of the kingdom. These successes, plus internal political turmoil in the Bijapur sultanate, spared Achyutadevaraya the fullness of the danger that had confronted Krishnadevaraya in 1509, though, like his brother, Achyutadevaraya had also to put down an uprising by Ummattur chiefs in southern Karnataka. So vigorous was Achyutadevaraya's defence of his throne that Rama Raja, after briefly sulking among kinsmen in Andhra, joined in the suppression of Chellappa's rebellion in 1531.

Within a few years, however, Rama Raja was again threatening, supported as before by the numerous, powerful progeny of his father and by two other adroitly contrived elements of strength. One was winning one of the Sakalaraju brothers from his alliance with Achyutadevaraya; the other was a windfall of military assistance. The last was an outcome of the serious internal conflicts that had rent Bijapur earlier and now resulted in a new sultan of Bijapur dismissing several thousand foreign Muslim soldiers who had opposed him. Rama Raja is reported to have immediately engaged these soldiers and made another bid to topple Achyutadevaraya in 1535.

Again, the king succeeded in parrying the challenge. One of the methods he adopted was to persuade some of the mightiest military commanders of the kingdom to make large and conspicuous donations to the god at Tirupati, Achyutadevaraya's tutelary, proclaiming their loyalty to him. Having twice mobilised and therefore divided the great men of the kingdom in contesting Achyutadevaraya's kingship, Rama Raja in the end succeeded in realising much of his ambition. After Achyutadevaraya's death in 1542, and possibly even before, Rama Raja became the virtual ruler of the country through Achyutadevaraya's young nephew and successor, Sadasivaraya, upon whom Rama Raja forced his regency.

During the middle of the sixteenth century, partly as a result of Rama Raja's machinations and partly as a result of deeper processes of which Rama Raja was a symptom, rather than a cause, extensive lordships were created throughout southern India. The agents and beneficiaries of this development were those military commanders whose service to Vijayanagara kings gave them the means to establish their own political places, a process which completed itself by the creation of a series of new kingdoms in the South: Mysore and Ikkeri in Karnataka and Gingee, Tanjavur and Madurai in Tamil country. Such state building had proceeded throughout the Vijayanagara period; ambitions for an englobing Vijayanagara over-lordship was never free from competitive political activities by great men of the time. That some of these activities resulted in dynastic changes after 1480 merely masked the deeper processes at work to frustrate the creation of a more centralised regime over all of the South. Opposing centralising forces were not only a host of ambitious men at all times, but still powerful community forces that biased political solutions to local rather than imperial levels of organisation.

The critical contribution of the Vijayanagara imperial order was precisely in weakening many ancient forms of communal organi-sation and allegiance and in empowering a whole new estate of warrior chiefs – some as military agents of the Rayas and some as local chiefs – to make political niches for themselves, often in opposition to the Vijayanagara rulers. Historians of the Vijayana-gara age have universally lamented the constant building of such anti-imperial centres; they mistakenly take as subversion of the Vijayanagara political order what was fundamental in the creation of that order during the fifteenth century as well as its destruction during the sixteenth century.

The old, south Indian medieval regime was actually finished by 1450, and a new kind of political structure had emerged as a result of the policies adopted by Devaraya II, an unrecognised architect of the Vijayanagara imperial order. His military improvements, based on the recruitment of Muslim fighters, set Vijayanagara on a path wholly different from that of all previous regimes in South India; his determination to control the major west coast ports from which war horses and trade treasure could be obtained was equally innovative; and his reliance upon and rewards to great military commanders, while temporarily strengthening his regime, created the new Vijaya-nagara generalissimos, men outside of the royal family whose capability as commanders gave them considerable, independent political standing. Moreover, Devaraya's opening to Muslim soldiers, his permission to construct mosques and cemeteries in the city, must shatter any remaining illusions of historians that the Hindu and dharmic ideology which may be attributed to the Sangama founders of the kingdom, continued to shape imperial policies. In the time of Devaraya, and later, the kingdom and the city came to represent a highly successful conquest state, indistinguishable from sultanates of the time and realised even more completely in the Maratha kingdom of the seventeenth and eighteenth centuries.

Saluva Narasimha crowned the transformation initiated by Devaraya II and in the process crowned himself. By checking the expansion of the Orissan Gajapatis into the wealthy coastal territory of the Krishna-Godavari delta and the Coromandel, he not only protected his Chandragiri patrimony, but set the stage for subjugation of the Tamil plain. His Tamil conquests differed from all previous Vijayanagara forays into the South by setting aside the ancient authority of Tamil kings and chiefs, whom he replaced by men like himself representing the new imperial order. Narasimha, like Devaraya II before him, also strove for more complete control of the west coast emporia to secure something of the trade wealth of the region and all of its imported war horses. His military successes against the Gajapatis and against Tamil foes came as the sons of Devaraya II (Mallikarjuna and Virupaksha II) quarrelled and fought each other, thus affording an opening for the political destiny that his vaulting reputation as military saviour of the kingdom promised. But even as Narasimha was achieving this, his own military commanders – Narasa Nayaka and Aravidi Bukka – were attaining something like the same status as generalissimos, thus creating the conditions where his new line of Vijayanagara kings was immediately placed in danger.

That Narasimha established a new kingship in 1485 but not a new and more secure capital as he might have, say at Chandragiri, indicates the widely held recognition of the city as the political centre of the entire South – the political capital had become political capital. Before its destruction in 1565, the city had come to symbolise a state that not only halted the advance of expanding Islam, but had extended its own authority over the whole of the South. For some time after its devastation, the city continued to stand for an exalted kingship to which lords throughout the southern peninsula offered homage and military service, if little else. But then, little else was really demanded beyond the homage that was owing to the great, conquering kings in their city that called itself 'Victory'.

FOUR

POLITICAL ECONOMY AND SOCIETY: THE SIXTEENTH CENTURY

The dharmic ideological impetus attributed to the formation of Vijayanagara in the fourteenth century was spent by 1450 when the reign of Devaraya II ended. Then, and thereafter, Vijayanagara was itself a successful conquest state, with much of Tamil country, Karnataka, and Andhra under Telugu and Kannadiga chiefs whose ruling authority was based upon military service to Vijayanagara kings. By the late fifteenth century, too, earlier, medieval political, social and economic institutions in the older settled, coastal parts of the southern peninsula had been weakened and no longer were the model of society that the Vijayanagara state had ostensibly been created to defend. Another system of politics, society, and economy had become ascendant, one that developed in the interior upland, on the dry and high Deccan plateau. The beneficiaries and major propagators of this new system were not only military servants of Vijayanagara kings, but local-level chieftains of Karnataka and Andhra who found new opportunities under the kingdom of Vijayanagara, which was now a conquest state.

In the previous chapter it was argued that while Vijayanagara military domination over the southern peninsula was established with surprising ease, the fiscal and political reach of the Rayas was both short and erratic. This loose suzerainty may account for part of the ease of the Vijayanagara conquest. What the sixteenth-century city on the Tungabhadra could command of the resources ostensibly available to its kings is neither precisely known nor knowable. There is not even the very generalized inventory of resources claimed as the political fruit of hegemony, such as that available for the Mughals in the *Ain i Akbari*, and surely, Vijayanagara claims to revenue came nowhere near what some scholars assume was available to the Mughals, that is, about 50 per cent of gross agrarian production. In the very heart of the Vijayanagara kingdom were numerous independent chiefs who, like the Mughal *mansabdar* and *jagirdar*, contributed troops and military leadership to imperial defence and aggression. However, the great chiefs of the Vijayanagara heartland were not royal officials whose military support could simply be commanded nor could they be transferred about from one prebend to another. A Vijayanagara chief was more like a Mughal *zamindar*, an autochthonous local lord of a domain that might be scattered over hundreds of square miles and therefore the bane of any overlord, whether Mughal or Vijayanagara, who sought a larger share of local resources and political tractability, dependence and order from local authorities.

The domains of such chiefdoms never appear to have had definite boundaries. Each chief, whether great or small, was identified by the central core of his authority around a major fortified town and often by a family name. The actual region under the domination of a chief was not, except at its core, a territory of consolidated power and authority. There are two important implications to be drawn from the dispersed character of political territories. One is that even the smallest chief could attempt to gain the protection of some distant great chief against another who might be closer. There appears to have been no conception of continuous territorial dominance at any level beyond certain ethnically defined cores, as a result of which great chiefdoms were mosaics of overlapping interests and hegemonies consisting of personal relations between some small magnate and a great one, and the durability of such relations could be fragile. The second implication stemming from this is that a conception of feudalism gains theoretical credibility. But there are still numerous reasons for rejecting the appropriateness of the feudal conception, among which the very high levels of exchange and commodity production is very important.

LORDSHIP AND COMMERCE

It has been shown that expanding, robust international trade was no more easy for the kings of Vijayanagara to tap for their uses than it was for the Mughals, in fact probably a good deal less easy. But this does not mean that there were no important consequences of the vigorous trade around India's coasts after 1500, during the 'Vasco da Gama era'. One major consequence was the substantial increase in money media which attended foreign trade of that time. All evidence points to the favourable trade balances of international trade for India and the settlement of these balances by bullion payments by foreign merchants. Only one commodity defied this practice. The importation of war-horses, known from the time of Marco Polo in the late thirteenth century, increased in volume and value during the Vijayanagara period, and so did imported cannon and hand guns. These war commodities were paid for by Indian exports and bullion according to the accounts of trade at the time. Weak additional support for this proposition comes from coin hoards, such as one of fourteenth-century coins found in Broach, on the western coast. Coins from everywhere in the Mediterranean and Indian Ocean were present in this find except for those from the horse-exporting Persian Gulf principalities. Apart from gold and silver hoarded or recast as personal or religious uses, most of the imported money media, including copper, and even cowries, added to the stock of money and made possible the expansion of money revenue demands everywhere in India and stimulated internal trade.

Great wealth could be had by those either directly involved in trade or politically positioned to take some portion of its rich proceeds. The review of trade and politics on the Kanara coast in the previous chapter leads to the conclusion that the major political beneficiaries of the rich trade there were local Hindu and Jaina chiefs during the sixteenth century.

But local Hindu and Jaina chiefs of the Kanara coast were not the only ones to benefit, as the recent research of Sanjay Subrahmanyam shows. Rajas on the Malabar coast south of Kanara also gained new resources from the increased trade of the sixteenth century and readily turned these resources into political assets. Others who found ways to convert trade wealth into political dominance were Muslims, among the most active traders. Ibn Batuta (d. 1377) mentioned one Jamal-ud-Din, son of a Goan shipbuilder and merchant, who used his family's trade wealth to hire an army of 6,000 and a fleet of over fifty ships. With these, he established himself as 'sultan' of Honavur, midway between the ports of Goa and Mangaluru. Jamal is said to have paid some tribute to Harihara I of Vijayanagara. By 1500, Portuguese records show that Honavur had reverted to Hindu rule, its chief paying tribute to Vijayanagara, but only after an invasion by Devaraya II. Another example of Muslim trade and political ascendency on the west coast is that of a

Mapilla (Muslim convert) trading family of Cannanore in Malabar who achieved a monopoly of trade with the Maldive Islands and thus of the coir ropes used by west coast ships between 1500 and 1530 by successfully fending off Portuguese interlopers.

Conditions on the eastern, or Coromandel, coast afforded no greater direct benefit to the Vijayanagara state. By the sixteenth century much of Coromandel trade was in the hands of Muslim traders – some Arabs, but mostly Marakkarar converts; others included Armenians and Portuguese deserters; the rest were Telugu Balija and Komati merchants who linked Pulicat with interior markets and production centres. In Pulicat, San Thome, or Naga-pattinam, according to foreign descriptions, which alone provide evidence on the matter, corporate groups managed the trade, administered the ports and collected the customs. The direct revenue benefit to the Rayas cannot have been high. However, the Rayas would have realised customs revenue as goods passed along the high roads connecting the principal Coromandel port at Pulicat and that of the Kanara coast, at Bhatkal, with the capital city.

The sixteenth-century population of the city, over 100,000, was an enormous magnet for consumer goods, and the routes connecting it with both coasts are reported to have had special military protection from Vijayanagara kings. Sixteenth-century Rayas sought stable and peaceful relations with the formidable newcomers to their shores, the Portuguese, from whom war goods came as well as desirable, exotic commodities for court consumption. It is not surprising to learn that despite conflicts between the Portuguese and traders on both coasts during Vijayanagara times, the trade was so valuable to the Portuguese that the defeat of the Rayas in 1565 was seen as a disaster. They feared that the victorious Deccan sultans might deny them a future place on the coasts because of their long-standing trade with Vijayanagara. Even more, however, the Portuguese feared that with the defeat of the Rayas general political conditions would decline everywhere and with that valuable trade.

Such fears were misplaced, as we now know. Defeat in 1565 did not end the resistance to Muslim expansion southward; this con-tinued with perhaps an enhanced place for the Portuguese. But, in the end, the trade hegemony that the Portuguese had wrestled from the Muslims during the sixteenth century was lost by them to other

Europeans: Dutch, British, and finally French. Moreover, the forces of commercialisation upon which the value of the Portuguese monopoly depended grew stronger throughout the sixteenth century, obedient to processes of which the Portuguese were not the cause. Among these processes were changing forms of lordship throughout the southern peninsula during the Vijayanagara era, not only in the coastal areas of high agriculture and 'high seas' commerce, but in the dry interior plateau above the coastal plains where political and economic changes had been quickening since the fourteenth century.

REGIONAL VARIATIONS IN THE KINGDOM

Tamil country was the major imperial frontier during the sixteenth century; the processes of change there are analysed in recent work of Karashima, Subbarayalu, and Ludden.

Karashima's analysis of interior sixteenth-century Arcot was intended as a contribution to a debate on feudalism in India. However, his findings defeat this objective. More significant than whether or not it is correct or useful to speak of 'feudalism' is his general finding about the continuity as well as the changes in ancient rights of established landed communities and their communal control over agrarian production and temples in the Arcot portion of the Tamil plain. He examined inscriptions found around the Vijayanagara strongholds of Padaividu and Gingee and, his speculations on feudalism apart, Karashima provides further documentation in support of Arjun Appadurai's explanation of how powerful outsiders, like Kannadiga warriors in this Tamil tract, strengthened their local suzerainty through mastery of temple affairs. This they accomplished by their endowments of lands and money, by their adjudication of conflicts among devotees and priests, and by encouraging, partly through example, the excavation of tanks and the improvement of water courses in temple villages. By these means, Karashima shows, Vijayanagara warriors received shares of valuable offerings of consecrated foodstuffs (*prasadam*) and other honours as benefactors and protectors of the gods, both of which fortified their ruling credentials. Temples having become major commercial centres also offered income from customs to locally powerful men for fostering and protecting these places.

Trade in the Arcot border country between the eastern ghats and the rich coastal agricultural zone was encouraged and exploited by soldier-agents of the Rayas and their local allies. The creation of markets (*pettai*) and fairs (*sandai*) was encouraged by tax concessions to those who settled in new market places: merchants, weavers, oil producers, betel sellers, and various artisans. Karashima even suggests that compulsion was used to increase production of cash crops such as sugar and pepper, another linkage between local production and international trade. Finally, he draws attention to the emergence of new landed groups, those who had no previous standing as landlords: Chettis, or merchants; Reddis, or soldiers; Kaikkolars, or weavers; and Manradis, or shepherds. These new entrants to local dominance displaced older groups, often adopting their titles, such as 'Natter'; they also undertook irrigation improvements with wealth acquired from trade, production and even office.

A companion study of the Vellar River valley in southern Arcot, by Karashima and Subbarayalu, provides a valuable comparative view of conditions of the fifteenth century with those of the sixteenth. By the earlier period, this part of the Tamil plain had been twice overrun by Vijayanagara soldiers who levied such high demands upon local cultivators, merchants, and artisans that they rose in revolt in 1429. Information on this uprising, said by Subbarayalu to be the first 'peasant revolt' in Tamil country, is drawn from inscriptions found in several places in the northern border country of the Kaveri basin. Alliances were formed among members of the two broad and usually conflicting groups of Tamil castes – right and left castes – to resist new demands by their conquerors. These included the introduction of a land measure disadvantageous to local cultivators, but there must have been other demands involving trade and production because local artisans and petty merchants of the left division of castes joined their traditional agrarian rivals of the right caste division in opposition.

Many of the conditions described in these analyses of late fifteenth- and sixteenth-century inscriptions from this area on the fringes of the Kaveri basin were replicated elsewhere in the southern Tamil plain. Foreign magnates – nayakas – closely involved in and benefiting from temple and market centres forged links with the older strata of local cultivators and merchants. Karashima distinguishes between certain features of adaptation to foreign warrior-rule by Tamils in the upper Vellar valley and those in the middle parts of the river basin. In the latter place, it was not so much warlord outsiders who exercised local dominance during the fifteenth century, but older locality authorities, in loose subordination to foreign warlords. These local magnates ruled in collaboration with a local soldiery, calling themselves 'Vanniyars' and drawn from Palli people from the nearby hill tracts. There were few foreign nayakas in the middle reaches of the Vellar during the fifteenth century; independent authority was exercised by local chiefs who added to their ancient title of 'Nattar' the more fashionable Tamil equivalent of 'Nayaka' (Tamil: *nayanar*) and they were not superseded by outsiders until well into the sixteenth century.

Ludden's research on Tirunelveli and on the relationship there between Vijayanagara conquerors from the north and older Tamil lordships of various kinds augments the findings of Karashima and Subbarayalu in the central Tamil plain. Pandyan rule over Madurai and Tirunelveli had progressively weakened from 1350 as a result of Muslim incursions as well as a brief revival of Chola power; this set the state for the imposition of Vijayanagara rule in 1550.

Among the Vijayanagara men who placed their stamp upon this far southern region was Saluva Narasimha. While still a loyal generalissimo, he rescued the goddess Andal from neglect by becoming a generous patron of her temple at Srivilliputtur, in a stroke bringing fame to himself and to the goddess. Another *vaduga*, or northerner, left a more permanent mark, because he and his family remained in Tirunelveli. This was Ettappa Nayaka. Beginning his rise as a warrior in the same Chandragiri that had nurtured Saluva Narasimha, Ettappa in 1423 led a band of followers to Madurai seeking service with the still independent, though weak, Pandyan king. By 1567, his descendants held a large domain of black-soil land in the eastern dry zone of the region and a fortress named Ettaiyapuram; this warrior family then cast its lot with Visvanatha Nayaka when the latter seized the governorship and established his independent rule over the territory. In addition to warriors like Ettappa and his successors, Telugu merchants and

Brahmans also joined the trek southward. All found places within the changing society of this region.

Tirunelveli town had been the southern capital of the Madurai Pandyan dynasty and the territory called Pandimandalam. The Nellaiappa temple there had been a royal shrine of the Pandyan kings of the thirteenth and fourteenth centuries, and it benefited from the royal support given for the construction of anicuts to extend irrigation from the Tambraparni. The enriched central Tambraparni river-basin was, and remained, under control of landed Brahman communities holding large, self-governing *brahmadeya* villages in alliance with members of the Vellalar cultivating community. When Pandyan royal authority was displaced in the sixteenth century by that of Vijayanagara commanders and other military adventurers from Andhra and by petty Maravar chieftains from the southern fringes of the Tambraparni basin, the central valley continued to be controlled by Brahman and Vellalar groups who enjoyed the right of *kani*, or communal ownership of land, as *kaniyatchikkaran*. Other migrants to Tirunelveli, like the Shanar palmyra-growers of Travancore and Maravar fighters from Ramnad, were also denied access to land in the central river-basin and therefore settled in the dry areas to the north and south of the valley. Neither they nor the Telugu conquerors themselves proved able to penetrate the Brahman-Vellalar monopoly over riverine fields, as a result of which Telugus settled on land in the eastern parts of the dry zone where they found black soils like those they left in their homeland. Interestingly, however, Telugu Brahmans along with Brahmans from Karnataka were permitted to join the Tamil Brahmans in the rich central plain, perhaps to preserve ancient Brahman privilege.

Lordships in sixteenth-century Tirunelveli reflected the distribution of its varied peoples in Vijayanagara times. The western foothills were settled by Maravars principally, and here a large number of Maravar *palaiyakkarar* were found; Telugu and Kannidigas settled the black-soil tracts in the eastern portion of the dry zone of the region and established many chieftaincies, including that of Ettaiyapuram. Even the lowly Shanars of Travencore were numerous enough to support a Shanar chiefdom in the south-eastern foothills. All of these chiefs passed under the hegemony of the

Nayaka kingdom of Madurai during the sixteenth century when Tirunelveli town served as a subsidiary capital as it had done in Pandyan times.

Sixteenth-century Andhra offers an instructive contrast to Tamil country in that local lordships, though powerful under the Golkonda sultans, enjoyed less independence than their counterparts in Tamil country under Vijayanagara. John Richards' monograph on Golkonda shows that Telangana had a political order very like that of Tamil country and Karnataka before the sixteenth century. From the Kakatiya period, when they held the major fortresses of the kingdom, Velama and Reddi 'warrior/cultivators' constituted a 'nobility' in Telangana and Rayalaseema, or northern and southern interior Andhra. They and their military followers first fought against, then joined, Muslim conquerors of Telangana. The ancient Velama/Reddi 'nobility' henceforward was a divided one, those of Telangana serving Muslim regimes and those of Rayalaseema, to the south, the Vijayanagara kings. Under the strong Qutb Shahi ruler Ibrahim (reign 1530–80), Reddi and Velama warriors found secure political niches. Ibrahim tempered military domination with considerable sympathy for Telugu culture acquired during a long stay in Vijayanagara as a political exile from his murderous brother. This together with his Telugu wife and the realities of politics encouraged the sultan to incorporate Telangana warrior chiefs into a single, Muslim-dominated political order. Moreover, state patronage of Brahmans and temples as well as Telugu poets continued. In characteristic Telugu royal style, encouragement was given to large and small tank-irrigation projects.

None of these measures would have been sufficient for a stable Golkonda regime had not Ibrahim also decided to leave the chiefs of Telangana with considerable autonomy in their ancient territories. Hence, when the challenge of Vijayanagara expansionism under Aliya Rama Raya occurred between 1542 and 1565, Golkonda's Telugu soldiery remained faithful to their Muslim ruler against the Hindu king, while their own kinsmen in Rayalaseema supported Vijayanagara. Until it was seized by the Mughals in 1687, the Golkonda political order remained unchanged. While Hindu chiefs ruled the countryside, the sultans built their new capital of Hyderabad in part from booty taken by Golkonda soldiers in the sack of

Vijayanagara in 1565. There, and at the old and strengthened fort of Golkonda, the sultan maintained their overlordship with a Muslim warrior aristocracy of heavy cavalrymen supported by a European artillery corps; the former held large lands for their maintenance, most realising their incomes through Hindu – mostly Brahman – bankers and tax-farmers. A royal monopoly of newly discovered diamonds gave the central regime the means of financing part of the new capital, paying mercenary artillery-men and buying their cannons, and supporting an elaborate court life. Diamond exports added to older valuable textiles in making Masulipatam the premier port on the Coromandel coast. That delta port eclipsed Pulicat, which faded quickly after the 1565 defeat of Vijayanagara, and by 1590, Masulipatnam rivalled the Mughal port of Surat on the west coast with whom it began to compete in the Indian Ocean trade.

The Muslim Golkonda regime rested on the collaboration of Telugu chiefs and Brahmans. Brahmans were the clerks of the central administration of the sultanate in Golkonda and its ubiquitous tax-farmers (Telugu: *sunkarulu*; Persian: *ijaradar*). Trade tolls and customs were left for others to collect; these were tax-farmers recruited from trade guilds whom the sultans, as the Kakatiya kings had before them, left free to manage their own trade and the ports where the trade was conducted. Telugu chiefs continued as before to be linked to others by ties of kinship marriage and interest. Under Golkonda, they continued to hold fortresses, but these were now under some Muslim control. To compensate for this these chiefs received royal honours from the Qutb Shahi court. As a locality 'aristocracy' drawn from 'Telugu warrior/cultivator castes', nayakas, and especially the greatest of their number, retained ancient chiefly authority. That was strengthened by their connection with a Muslim kingdom, more powerful than any predecessors because of its Muslim cavalrymen and its European gunners, and more centralised than the Vijayanagara kingdom, hence its prebendalism correspondingly stronger. By the sixteenth century, differences between Hindus and Muslims were no more a barrier to political collaboration in Golkonda than they were in Vijayanagara.

Local lordship in Karnatak was different from that of sixteenth-century Golkonda in the greater independence of chiefs from central authority and thus its weaker prebendal forms. During the fifteenth and sixteenth centuries, the plain, or *maidan*, of southern Karnataka was nominally under an agent of the Vijayanagara kings whose headquarters was the fortress at Srirangapatman in the upper Kaveri. This agent, often dignified by historians with the title of 'viceroy', was responsible for collecting tribute from surrounding chiefs, usually calling themselves *odeyar*, of whom one was the chief of what became Mysore town, ten miles from Srirangapatnam. There were other such chiefs in this part of the upper Kaveri valley which was destined to become the core of the seventeenth-century Mysore kingdom. On the northern boundary of the future core of that kingdom was the area called Morasu-nadu (modern Bangalore and Tumkur districts) dominated by one of the large sections of the southern Karnatak peasantry, Morasu Vokkaligas, who seemed to have been Telugu migrants to the area in the fourteenth century. To the south of the core of the future Mysore state was Kongu with its mixed population of Kannadigas, Telugus, and principally Tamils; to the east and north-east there were Telugu chieftains the most powerful of whom was the lord of Mulbagal.

Odeyars (or 'wodeyars', to add the Dravidian phonological glide) of Mysore arose as minor chiefs during Vijayanagara times; they are first glimpsed in the early sixteenth century in a Kannada literary work of the time of the chief Chamaraja (1513–53), purportedly a local subordinate of Achyutadevaraya. Chamaraja's domain began as a handful of villages along the Kaveri where he established a small fortified place called Mahisura-nagara (from which Maisur and Mysore). The first inscriptions of these modest chiefs came in the time of Timmaraja Wodeyar, in 1551. By the 1570s the chieftaincy had expanded to thirty-three villages protected by a force of 300 soldiers, and in 1610, the last of the Vijayanagara agents at Srirangapatanam sold the fortress to Raja Wodeyar (1578–1617) under whom the chiefdom expanded into a major principality.

A more powerful chiefly family there during the sixteenth century was that of Yelakanda in the northern part of modern Bangalore district. This was a chiefdom established by Tamil warriors who migrated from the Kanchi region in the early fifteenth century and served in Vijayanagara armies. Most famous of these chiefs was Kempe Gowda who assumed the chieftaincy from his father in 1513.

The modest origin of this family is preserved in the title 'gowda', usually meaning 'village headman', a lineage title used by the family founder, Jaya Gowda. His descendant Kempe seems to have been responsible for the expansion of a modest chiefly patrimony. During the time of Krishnadevaraya villages were added to the family's holdings around Yelakanda, doubling its area, and in the time of Achyutadevaraya, Kempe Gowda founded the fortified town of Bangaluru and gathered to himself yet more villages. Kempe enlarged Bangaluru in the time of Sadasivaraya, building several tanks and temples; he also began to mint his own coins then and possibly joined with other Karnatak chiefs in opposing the Rayas in the late 1550s, perhaps objecting to Aliya Rama Raya's deposition of Sadasivaraya. For the last (but not his other aggrandisements) Kempe served some years in prison before being ransomed and released. Shortly after, in 1569, he died.

Vijayanagara kings endeavoured to maintain some authority over the chiefs of southern Karnataka from several fortified places there that were entrusted to members of the royal family or to loyal soldiers. This proved difficult as a result of which their overlordship was weak even in this region close to the kingdom's heartland. The frustrations of their overlordship are exemplified by their relations with the Ummattur chiefs of Sivasamudram. These chiefs carried on unceasing aggression against neighbours even though subjected to punitive expeditions from the time of Narasa Nayaka, after he seized the throne in 1497, and Krishnadevaraya from 1510 to 1512, as already noted. Even after the brilliant military successes of the first years of his reign, Krishnadevaraya was unable to end Ummattur influence in southern Karnataka, for he appointed the son of Gangaraja, the Ummattur chief he had defeated in a difficult campaign, to rule over Srirangapatanam, and descendants of that family held this fortress until it was yielded to Raja Wodeyar in 1610.

Besides the chiefs of Ummattur and Mysore who bore the title of odeyar, there were others in southern Karnataka who maintained their independent rule through most of the sixteenth century.

In northern Karnataka there was an even more impressive chiefly house that arose in Vijayanagara times and came to enjoy an extensive sovereignty. These were the Keladi chiefs who later founded the Nayaka kingdom of Ikkeri. At its greatest, the Ikkeri rajas controlled a territory nearly as large as the Vijayanagara heartland, some 20,000 square miles, extending about 180 miles south from Goa along the trade-rich Kanara coast.

The Keladis emerged from obscurity in the decade before Krishnadevaraya's reign. Then, a young farmer-become-warrior chief, one Chauda, distinguished himself in service under a Vijayanagara commander, on the strength of which he strove to create a domain of his own. Divine intervention provided him with the means to build a fort and add to his followers; this was in the form of a treasure-trove pointed out by a goddess as other divines had yielded the same knowledge to Kempe Gowda, another peasant man, and to a young shepherd who founded the Gingee chiefdom in Tamil country. Chauda's metamorphosis was completed in January 1500, when he installed himself as Chaudappa Nayaka of the Keladi Mula Samasthan (the pivotal great house of Keladi) and consecrated a temple dedicated to Siva. He served Achyutadevaraya faithfully during the latter's travails against Chellappa and Rama Raya and was rewarded in 1535 with the governorship of Barakuru and Mangaluru on the Kanara coast at the base of the ghats on which his domain was.

Chaudappa Nayaka's son ruled as Sadasiva Nayaka from about 1540 to 1565. He moved to a higher level of lordship as a commander of the Rama Raja army that humiliated the Bijapur sultans in southern Maratha country by seizing the fortresses of Ahmednagar and Gulbarga. As a reward, the Vijayanagara king granted him the title 'Sadasivaraya Nayaka', and for his later military services he was granted the title of 'Raja Nayaka' and the same Kanara governorship previously enjoyed by his father. Under such royal sponsorship, he began to assume direct control over contiguous tracts of poligar holdings and thereby extended his realm over all of Tulu country and much of neighbouring Shimoga, or Araga. To temple building, close relations with the Sringiri *matha*, endowments to Jaina and Virasaiva shrines, military service to Vijayanagara, and local conquests that enlarged his realm, Sadasivaraya Nayaka of Ikkeri added the royal activity of founding new towns and markets. He created the pilgrimage centre of Sadasivapura in honour of the king or himself, we cannot know. This was a Brahman settlement, or *agrahara*, to which the Raja added the usual privileges to attract merchants and artisans who would make it into a rich revenue resource for himself and his successors; privileges included deferring customs collections for some years and permission for merchants to build warehouses and residences around the bazaar street as well as providing special quarters for various artisan-traders. Though a palace was also constructed in Sadasivapura, he promised that there would be no royal interference in the town's government by its Brahman and merchant residents. Another new chiefdom of the sixteenth century arose at the eastern margins of Karnataka, at Lapakshi. This was founded by three sons of a merchant of that town. They, like their contemporaries at Keladi, rose to prominence as soldiers in the armies of the rayas, bringing fame and fortune to their natal town through their military exploits during the sixteenth century. As commanders, and later as provincial governors, they deployed their royal rewards to create a substantial patrimony around Lapakshi and to make the town one of the great Siva pilgrimage centres of the century. One of the three, Virapanayya Nayaka, became governor of Penukonda-rajyam on whose southern borders Lapakshi was situated; his capital during the reign of Achyutadevaraya was Gooty according to a 1529 inscription. Other brothers held offices under the same king in the fortress of Chitradurga. All were devoted Virasaivas, as were the Keladi chiefs, and all established and supported Virasaiva mathas or seminaries wherever they held authority in the Kannada–Telugu border country.

THE ANATOMY OF SIXTEENTH-CENTURY CHIEFDOMS

Chiefs such as these attained fame and wealth as leaders of military contingents in the service of Vijayanagara kings of the fifteenth and sixteenth centuries. As benefactors of temples and as town builders, they are mentioned in inscriptions of the time. However, most of the South Indian countryside was ruled by chiefs of a more modest sort, who would have been totally lost to history except for accounts of them gathered by Mackenzie during the early nineteenth century.

Among the most important revelations of the Mackenzie collection are those pertaining to administration. Just as coercive means were widely distributed among a large stratum of territorial and local magnates, so were administrative capabilities; military fiscalism and modest bureaucraticisation was not imposed from above, by royal officials for example, it arose from the base of the political system, from its many chiefs, its numerous villages, and its temples.

Three modes of administration converged to form a single general form during the fifteenth and sixteenth centuries. One Mackenzie identified as the corps of Brahman accountants and scribes serving great imperial households: those of royal lineages and great commanders of the rayas. As both of these kinds of households moved from the Deccan heartland of the kingdom into the south, they were accompanied by Brahman coadjutors, either Deshastas from northern Karnataka or Niyogi Brahmans from Andhra. The latter groups gathered information on villages and towns under the expanding authority of their warrior masters and negotiated the relationships betweeen the latter and the Brahman-dominated temples with whom these Vijayanagara agents sought to create an enduring conquest. Resource inventories would have been obtained by agents of the Rayas from several sources which together constituted other modes of existing administration, that of village and locality organisations as well as managers of temples. Records of landholdings and of shops and artisanal producers were maintained by village accountants (e.g. Tamil: *nattukaranam* or Telugu: *despandya*). Most were Brahmans, though in Tamil country they could also be Vellalars or Pillais.

One surviving administrative record of resources is for the town of Aluvakonda, or Alamkonda (modern Kurnool district), dating from 1563.[1] This was an inventory prepared when the town was granted as an entitlement to income for military service, or *amaram*, by one Rangapparajaya to a subordinate. This Rangapparajaya seems to have been an important chief in the Rayalaseema judging from his land gifts to the nearby Vaishnava shrine of Ahobalam at the time. According to an account collected by Mackenzie in 1800, Aluvakonda was founded by some shepherd chiefs calling themselves 'Yadava Rajas' and was enlarged and fortified during the early fifteenth century by a chief named Gaurappa Nayudu. Gaurappa's

---

[1] K. A. Nilakanta Sastri and N. Venkataramanayya, *Further Sources in Vijayanagara History* (Madras: University of Madras, 1946); vol. 3, pp. 121–6.

grandson became a rebel against the new Tuluva kings as a result of which Vira Narasimharaya (reign 1505–9), Krishnadevaraya's older brother and predecessor, seized Aluvakonda, razed its fort, and killed its chief. An inventory of the town and chieftaincy of twelve villages was prepared at that time. Its comprehensiveness and detail offers strong testimony of the quality of administration available to even moderate chiefs of the time.

According to the inventory, the total money income realisable from rents and fees was 4,460 gold coins (*gadyana*, a coin of 52 grains). About three-quarters of this total money revenue can be accounted from the following sources. Dry fields around the town were rented by eighteen different people whose money payments comprised a mere 9 per cent of the total income of the town while the few wet fields yielded a small money rent and some paddy. Thirty-nine shops were enumerated in the town, and these were owned by four men: the previous chieftain Gaurappa owned nine of them; two, possibly Balija Chetti Telugu merchants, owned six each, another man owned six, while the remaining twelve shops were owned by smaller Balija Chettis. It was noted that seven of the shops paid no rent while the rest paid an aggregate rent of 53 gold coins, about 1 per cent of the total rental value of the chieftaincy. Looms were subject to a tax and some 400 were reported in the town. Of these, half produced red cloth for sale in the bazaar established by and named for Gaurappa Nayudu, Gaurappayanipeta. Forty-one of the looms paid no tax; the remainder paid the cash equivalent of 5 per cent of the total income, and weavers of the town additionally paid a perquisite (*vartana*) to Gaurappa as well as a smaller payment to support the fort that he had built. Herdsmen of the area contributed taxes equal to 4 per cent of the total income; and certain groups paid *jati siddhya*, a small communal, or caste tax. The largest single source of the town's revenue was from betel traders, oil millers, money changers, liquor makers, cotton cleaners, and indigo producers, who paid 1,217 gold coins, or 27 per cent of the total. The chiefdom's twelve dependent villages contributed about a quarter of its total income. Of those villages that can be identified now, several were quite distant from Aluvakonda, two being around 50 miles away, thus good examples of the scattered interests of contemporary chiefdoms. Each of these villages under protection of the Aluvakonda chiefs seemed to have met its obligations by payments from a head merchant (*pedda setti*), perhaps for the shops in and around the tributary village, from a headman of local herders (*golla*), and from a cultivator headman (*reddi*). By the late sixteenth century, when Aluvakonda was reassigned to the military dependent of Rangapparayaya, its annual rental and tax income had increased four-fold and the villages under its domination had risen to forty-three. The wealth of this chieftaincy had now become large enough for 10,000 gold coins to be alienated for the benefit of Brahmans and temples.

Of sixteenth-century chiefdoms, Aluvakonda was neither large nor important; its administrations would have been dwarfed by those of the great chieftaincies in the Rayalaseema region of Andhra or some parts of Tamil country and Karnataka. Fortified and commercial places like Gandikota in the hilly Cuddapah countryside of the middle course of the Penner River, or Nandyal, 30 miles from Aluvakonda in Kurnool, were the seats of great chiefly houses at the time. Another such place was Anantapur town which was called 'Hande Anantapur' until well into the nineteenth century, an acknowledgement of the dominance of the Hande family whose authority reached over a large part of Rayalaseema. The chief Rangapparajya who held Aluvakonda is said to have been a dependent of the Hande *samasthanam*. The Pemmasani family of Gandikota and Nandyala chiefs were part of the widely ramified coalition of Aliya Rama Raja and contributed to the latter's overwhelming power in the middle of the sixteenth century; they continued long after Rama Raja's time to hold great power in the erstwhile eastern heartland of the Vijayanagara kingdom. Controlling numerous villages and many large towns, these powerful chiefs commanded large mercenary armies that were the vanguard of Vijayanagara forces during the sixteenth century. While we have no records of their administrations, they would have had to be quite substantial.

Equally complex and elaborate administrative organisation would have been found at temples, especially larger ones, during the sixteenth century. One of the largest was that at Tirupati, 125 miles south-east of Aluvakonda and set like it at the edge of a range of hills on one of whose crests was Tirumalai, the major shrine of the god Venkatesvara. Between 1450 and 1550, the Tirupati-Tirumalai temple complex became the most important pilgrimage and sectarian centre in all of the south. This makes it a unique temple, no doubt, but the causes of its development were shared by many temples of the time.

Two factors account for the transformation of this small, ancient shrine into a teeming centre of pilgrimage and political influence. One was the patronage of political notables, in this case Saluva Narasimha, whose Chandragiri headquarters was nearby. The second factor was the irrigation investments by managers of the temple (*sthanattar*) in lands donated to the god. Both factors came into operation at the same time. The first recorded irrigation investment of a money endowment in a Tirupati temple village dates from 1454, when a Brahman priest of Chandragiri gave 3,000 gold coins (*panam* of about six grains of gold each) to the temple to provide a daily food offering for twelve other Brahmans. This endowment specified that the money be used to excavate irrigation channels in temple villages and that part of the higher crop yields from this investment was to provide the specified food offering. The Chandragiri Brahman donor was most likely an agent of Saluva Narasimha and a sect leader since the beneficiaries of the grant were a group of Brahmans who otherwise performed no services at the temple; hence this provides another instance of how funds passed from a powerful lord to a sectarian leader and from him to a temple conferring merit and honour on both. In 1456, Saluva Narasimha made the first of many endowments in his own name to the Tirupati temple by granting a village free of all taxes.

Subsequently he and his successors to the Vijayanagara throne enlarged their support to the temple, royal endowments reaching a high point in the time of Achyutadevaraya. In the middle of the 1530s, numerous endowments for the merit of the king were made. This reflected more than Achyutadevaraya's personal allegiance to Venkatesvara, whose protection he had sought and before whom he was crowned after the death of his brother, Krishnadevaraya. These large endowments by royals and their military servants may have been intended as a public acknowledgement of support for the king in his struggle against Aliya Rama Raja. Between 1530 and 1542, a total of thirty-nine different land grants resulted in the alienation of income from forty-three villages for the benefit of the Tirupati temple as well as the donation of nearly one-half million small gold coins. Achyutadevaraya's rival, Rama Raja, when he was the power behind Sadasivaraya's throne, after Achyutadevaraya had died, granted sixty villages and 190,000 small gold coins to the god Venkatesvara.

By Rama Raja's death in 1565, which marked the end of Vijayanagara greatness and of much of its munificence, the Tirupati temple held 170 villages of which about one hundred had received some sort of irrigation investment from money endowments. All of the transactions – the original gift of a temple village and the subsequent investment in irrigation improvements – were punctiliously recorded and supervised by temple authorities. Accountants of the temple (there were thirteen according to an inscription of 1546) maintained the elaborate accounts necessary to ascertain that the offerings for which endowments had been made – usually the presentation of cooked foods to a deity – were carried out. This meant organising the food-stuffs and supervising their preparation in the kitchens of the temple, then seeing to it that the valuable consecrated food was distributed to various named beneficiaries in accordance with the terms of the endowment as recorded in an inscription. All of these arrangements required the attention of a very large set of temple servants, from treasury officials to a public works department to carry out irrigation improvements. It is difficult to conceive that even the Vijayanagara kings maintained an administrative capability much more elaborate than some temples with their extensive holdings of land, their hundreds of priests and other employees, including scribes, engravers, accountants, and irrigation specialists.

Accountants, scribes, and bankers constituted an administrative infrastructure supporting all major lordships of the later Vijayanagara age. This was a diverse structure of authority, ranging from the highest level of Vijayanagara kings and collateral members of ruling lineages, and the most trusted military commanders in a descending order of lordships to village headmen. All depended on record-keepers and other administrative ancillaries including money specialists, from minters of coins to handlers of bills through whom tribute was transferred over long distances. Local accountants and scribes, as well as money men, were essential links between the variety of lordly recipients of wealth and the productive base that they exploited. Administrative specialists provided a web upon which the entire fabric of Vijayanagara politics was intricately woven.

KINGS AND CHIEFS

The fragmentary character of Vijayanagara politics and society could be ameliorated, but not overcome, by any administrative structure as long as lordship itself continued to be segmentary. Every magnate, large or small, exploited all within his political sphere so as to maintain or increase his power with respect to aggressive neighbouring lords and so as to increase his standing with the warlords whom all were under pressure to serve. Vijayanagara political relations had none of the remedies for fissiparous and fragmented lordship thought to be found elsewhere in India. There was nothing of what many scholars of Mughal society presume in their conception of a patrimonial-bureaucratic state or that some students of Vijayanagara history presume in their conception of a feudal Vijayanagara. Lordship in Vijayanagara times was shaped by different factors. Some of these operated at all levels of sixteenth-century society, including village society; other factors are to be found specifically in political relationships, including those between Vijayanagara lords and Muslim regimes north of the Vijayanagara kingdom. The first set of these factors impinging on Vijayanagara lordship are explored in the remaining pages of the present chapter; the second will be dealt with in the following chapter.

At the highest level of lordship, competition within and among royal lineages for the throne set a limit on the degree of centralised power attainable in the absence of the sort of imperial military and administrative corps of foreigners that could serve as the flywheel of the contemporaneous Mughal polity. Yet, even in the Mughal regime, succession struggles and even assassinations occurred as they did in the Vijayanagara kingdom, where the threat of violent death and usurpation at the hand of some relative or military commander was ever present. Candidates for the Vijayanagara throne maintained coalitions of supporters who were always ready to resist counter-coalitions and any effort toward centralisation. Indeed, at the very outset of the kingdom, it is uncertain whether there was one or five kingdoms. Each of the sons of Sangama ruled seemingly as a governor, or *mahamandelesvara*, except that there was no sovereign and each ruled over a rajya, or kingdom, on the various frontiers of Karnataka.

How it was that Bukka I emerged as supreme cannot be reconstructed now, but it was his sons and their descendants that became the main royal line for the remainder of the first dynasty. This created a more powerful, single kingship, but one that was rarely free from deadly competition from agnatic and collateral kinsmen of disinherited princes. Five assassinations and four usurpations occurred before the Sanagama line itself was displaced by Saluva Narasimha in 1486; hence Narasimha's action was an innovation in only one sense – it signalled the claim for sovereignty by great commanders of the kingdom. Even this opening of the throne to military talent beyond the royal line was anticipated in the time of Devaraya II when enlarged royal mercenary forces began to confer major power and influence upon commanders, transforming them into generalissimos with considerable independent political standing.

This was an important change in political forces at the imperial level. It added to the already complex mosaic of great houses, with their overlapping claims and conflicts, an enhanced power for some who, by virtue of leadership of the best armies of the time, were able to advance their own territorial interests against the claims of rivals and monarchs alike. Thus Saluva Narasimha assiduously expanded his patrimonial base in Chandragiri to include much of the northern Tamil plain of Tondaimandalam before he seized the throne. Later, Aliya Rama Raja's leading commanders of the Pemmasani, Hande, and Nandyala families did the same over much of Rayalaseema and Telangana. The proximity and overlappings of territories of these major allies of Rama Raja meant that as each strove against the others to gain land and followers, and there was no way to ascertain the boundaries of any. Boundaries, in fact, mattered less than the personal relations between a great and a small chief, however separated in space they might be; protection in return for military service guided political relations, and these relations were as firm, or as fluid, as personalities and circumstances dictated.

However, in the manner of segmentary political forms anywhere, competing chiefs combined when their overlord called upon them and when it was in their interests to do so. This happened during Rama Raja's two challenges to Achyutadevaraya, in 1530 and 1535; it happened again when Rama Raja launched his expansionist drive across the Tungabhadra and called upon his client chiefs to lead the assault against the sultanates there. This Vijayanagara thrust inevitably produced a similar combination among the Muslim regimes that had superseded the Bahmani sultans, for Rama Raja so threatened the sultanate regimes as to force them to set aside long-standing conflicts to defeat their common Hindu enemy in 1565.

The first Tuluva kings, Vira Narasimha and his brother Krishnadevaraya, appeared determined to bring the great chiefs of the realm to heel, possibly because of the widespread opposition to them from Karnatak and Tamil chiefs. It is not at all clear what prompted this opposition around the turn of the sixteenth century. It is probable that the fratricidal conflict among the last of the Sangamas led to the development of factional coalitions among powerful houses in Andhra and Karnataka and encouraged many to pursue aggrandising objectives that depended on a weak central authority. Saluva Narasimha quelled some of that by the sheer weight of his military power, but the coalition building that led to the replacement of his son as king reopened the arena of conflict among ambitious chiefs. This may explain the vehemence of Vira Narasimha's suppression of the Aluvakonda chiefdom and the determination with which Krishnadevaraya broke the back of the Ummattur-led rebellion of southern Karnatak chiefs. He then went further and developed a more comprehensive strategy than punishing errant chiefs; he sought to create a more certain monopoly of force under royal control based, as already noticed, on the fuller use of Brahman agents, royal fortresses under Brahman commanders, and garrison as well as local militia forces recruited from among the tough forest people of the peninsula, his poligars.

The Telugu didactic poem, *Amuktamalyada*, said to have been composed by Krishnadevaraya commends Brahmans as provincial governors and fortress commenders because their first loyalty would be to the king and because they would strive to overcome the disdain of Kshatriya and Sudra officers. Forest fighters, Boyas or

Bedars, were commended as valuable shock troops and plunderers during military campaigns and as dependable garrison forces. The principal object to be achieved was the reduction of independent chiefs:

> That king can lay his hand on his breast and sleep peacefully who appoints as masters of his fortresses such Brahmins as are attached to himself, are learned in many sciences and arts, are addicted to *dharma*, are heroic and have been in ... service since before his time ... [and] who give to the subordinate chiefs (*samanta*) lands and other things without lessening in the slightest the degree of arrangement with them ... [while] minding the (small) faults of the forest chiefs ... [without] extensive power is like trying to clean a mud wall by pouring water over it. If ... [the king] gets angry with them he cannot destroy them utterly. If (on the other hand) he attaches them to himself by kind words and charity they would be useful to him in invading foreign territory and plundering their fortresses ...[2]

Royal retribution for the sedition or insubordination of chiefs became canonised in the late sixteenth-century Telugu poem, the *Rayavachakamu*, which recalled the reign of Krishnadevaraya. There the king confided to his trusted Brahman minister, Appaji, a desire to visit 'those kingdoms, forts, countries, strongholds, Visnu shrines, the estates of subordinate chiefs and the frontiers' of the kingdom he had received from his brother, father, and grandfather. Appaji and other ministers approved:

> One should tour the country ruled over by one's ancestors. Nothing can be known if one remains stationary ... it is necessary that the people ... should know Your Majesty ... establish your glory by touring the kingdom in all dirctions, accompanied by the four-fold army so as to create terror in the mind of enemies and subordinate chiefs.[3]

Launching a *digvijaya*, or tour of conquest, was conventional advice, of course, but there is more meaning in the verse than that. This is the notion that personal rule must be established over all chiefs. The Marathi text of governance of a century or so after, the *Ajnapatra* speaks a similar language of suspicion toward local chiefs

[2] Rangasvami Sarasvati, 'Political Maxims of the Emperor-Poet Krishnadeva Raya', *The Journal of Indian History* 4, part 3 (1925), p. 72.

[3] K. A. Nilakanta Sastri and N. Venkataramanayya, *Further Sources in Vijayanagara History* (Madras: University of Madras, 1946), vol. 3, p. 141.

who, while appearing to accept a royal overlordship, actually resort to dissension (*bheda*) to make any lordship difficult since chiefs are ever concerned to protect their hereditary rights of rule and possession (*vatan*) against royal or prebendal demands. Neither the Telugu *Rayavachakamu* nor the Marathi *Ajnapatra* offer solutions to the conflict of interests between kings and chiefs beyond a personal relationship of dominance over a chief either directly by the king or through a personal agent of the king (*karyakarta*). Failure to achieve such a relationship meant a loss of prestige and tribute to the king and the risk to the chief of royal chastisement if a demand for tribute or troops was not met.

This was an age when all lordships from the king to even the most modest chief were becoming more powerful. Greater militarisation, more lethal arms, larger treasuries based upon the expanding commerce of the time, and more efficient fiscal controls assured that this would be true. And, because all lordships – the great and the small – strengthened themselves simultaneously and in the same ways, the hazards to all increased simultaneously. Yet there were constraints upon the powers that could be garnered to any lord as already noticed in the case of the kings themselves and some of the great chiefs. Other constraints upon lordships came from below.

THE SOUTH INDIA 'COMMONS'

Local politics and property relations, whether in the riverine zones of ancient, high agriculture or in the extensive areas of dry-cropping, were founded on corporate control, either of communal holders of special privileges, usually Brahmans and temples, or of corporate landed lineages. Private landed proprietorship did not exist in its modern meaning, though it is assumed by Karashima and Subbarayalu on the evidence of land transfers among individuals dating from Chola times. In most cited instances, the acquisition of land by a chief was preliminary to making a gift to some Brahmans, a temple, or a *matha*; thus, they were special cases of chiefly prerogative. Invariably, such records are temple inscriptions and therefore pertain to gifts; if non-religious sales of land were common during the sixteenth century, or before, there is no way of knowing it. However, because such transactions of which there are records were intended to enhance the ruling credentials of chiefs in accordance with prevailing notions of *rajadharma* or *dana* (gift), it should not be overlooked that religious endowments resulted in various kinds of advantage for the chiefly donor besides public esteem and religious merit. In many temples, donors were entitled to portions (as much as a quarter) of the offerings to a god, *prasadam*; this was valuable and could be gifted or sold. Chiefly and royal donors also sought and received administrative and judicial rights in temples which conferred material and status benefits. Hence, in rejecting Karashima's claim that private proprietorship of land is attested by gifting activities, it is recognised that substantial material benefits were nevertheless obtained by the great donors of the age.

Still, the underlying communal character of landholding during Vijayanagara times cannot be questioned, nor is it by Karashima and Subbarayalu. The political power arising from the communal organisation and ideology of leading sections of dominant landed castes on irrigated coastal tracts was very great; this included Brahmans, Tamil Vellalars, Kannadiga Vokkaligas, and Telugu Reddis. But no less great was that of the major landholding groups in the interior upland frontier during the sixteenth century, when the same high degree of communal property and politics existed, but it was differently constituted.

The dry-cropping zones between about 1,000 and 3,000 feet over the coastal plain constantly expanded; this was the agricultural and political frontier of Vijayanagara times. Many of the new settlers were migrants from the coasts, such as the Reddis of Telangana and Rayalaseema, for example. However, others who opened new tracts of field agriculture were those who previously lived by herding combined with extensive dry-cropping and even slash-and-burn cultivation in the still heavily-forested upland. Dry lands of the interior had to be conquered by an armed peasantry under fighting chiefs if they were to be held against the opposition of conquered cultivators and herdsmen.

Thus, scattered over the uplands of Andhra, Karnatak, and Tamil country were mixed communities of farmers and herdsmen ruled by fighting chiefs. These were not an easy people for any would-be centralising regime, as that of Krishnadevaraya, to subdue, dominate, and from whom to realise much financial or political benefit.

Here, communal property and privilege was defended partly by the fighting capabilities of martial peasantries, but against larger and more persistent external foes, such opposition could take other forms. One was the convening by village and locality headmen of a *kuttam*, or assembly, of cultivating and other groups of a locality to agree measures for opposing demands from above. Resistance could range from the withholding of money dues to an overlord to a temporary abandonment of villages for the refuge of forests until negotiations led to a satisfactory settlement of differences. Assemblies of this sort are known from the fifteenth century, as noted above in connection with peasant opposition in Tiruchirappalli in 1429–30; they continue to be reported in the eighteenth and nineteenth centuries as an established means of coping with oppression from above as well as of settling serious internal disputes. Desertion of their lands was a last answer to oppression by dry-zone cultivators; it was often not difficult for these motile cultivators to obtain other lands and possibly less demanding masters elsewhere. Thus, dry-zone cultivators were armed against oppressors by more than their spears (and increasingly their matchlock guns). Cultivation skills, material resources, and organisation for teasing food and commodities like cotton from harsh soils gave them mobility and an ability to bargain favourable terms as valuable additions to ambitious lords anywhere, for more men, especially potential fighting men, meant more political and economic power.

In all of these upland communities were found administrative offices such as village and locality headmen, usually filled by members of the dominant landholding groups, village and locality accountants, usually Brahmans, and a variety of lesser offices. All were remunerated by chiefly grants of tax-exempt land holdings – frequently from scarce irrigated holdings – designated by the Sanskrit word, *manya*, which implies an honour as well as an income. This method of paying for local administration was continued by the British in the interior districts of Madras Presidency; the landholdings in lieu of money payment for village and locality officials were then called by the Arabic term *inam*, and these were continued until well into the nineteenth century, even though such privileged landholdings might comprise as much as half of all cultivated land.

The riverine valleys of Tamil country had neither local chiefs nor even village headmen. Vijayanagara kings themselves were far less evident here, or in deltaic Andhra, than they were in the spacious interior upland of the peninsula judging from the relatively few Vijayanagara inscriptions found in the wet zones. In areas of ancient high agriculture, local authority was held by corporate bodies rather than poligars or village and locality headmen. Groups of prestigious holders of land rights, such as those in Tamil country, were called *kaniyatchikkaran*, or collective hereditary land owners. During the colonial epoch, when such communal holders in irrigated zones were dubbed with the Persianised title of 'mirasidar', they proved as resistant to the centralising aspirations of the British as they had done to the Vijayanagara state and their successors, the nayaka kings of Tanjavur (1530–1680) and of the Maratha Rajas of Tanjavur (1680–1800).

In the irrigated central valley of the Tambraparni, Ludden notes the absence of village or locality headmen, accountants, and watchmen in early inscriptions. Nineteenth-century reports confirm this. Older inscriptional sources without exception place local authority over these most valuable irrigated villages in the hands of a communal élite of Brahmans and Vellalars. Such village services as they required were paid for in cash, just as they paid for the services of fighters to defend their wealth from external predators with the temerity to challenge the landed wealth that went with high ritual status. By the sixteenth century, communal land holding was strengthened through other forms of wealth and influence: involvement in the trade of grain, and scribal and accountancy offices held in the regional regimes in the river valleys. Altogether, these holders of the *kani*-right were 'the government of the wet zone, not only at the village level . . . [but as a] subregional ruling class', as Ludden states.

How the ancient privileges of the wet-zone élite could have survived the penetrations of martial Vijayanagara requires explanation. There appear to be several reasons for it. The river valleys of the peninsula yielded the most reliable tribute to Nayaka agents of the kingdom because of their large, annual surplus production. Providing that the appointed Vijayanagara agent was loyal, money tribute was transferred to Vijayanagara. Such was the case under Kumara Kampana in the fourteenth century and when Chellappa

Saluva Narasimha Nayaka served Krishnadevaraya in the Kaveri valley.

But, Chellappa ceased sending tribute and threatened the entire kingdom by his revolt in 1531. So great were the resources available to him that Achyutadevaraya mobilised the rest of the kingdom to suppress this Tamil wet-zone revolt. Achyutadevaraya's hold on the throne was tenuous then as a result of the machinations of Aliya Rama Raja and his powerful coalition of Rayalaseema chiefs. Hence the decisiveness of his response to Chellappa's sedition indicates how critical this challenge was seen to be. Moreover, Rama Raja shared this view for he temporarily suspended his active opposition to the king during the revolt in the southern peninsula.

Even with the most reliable subordinates and agents, it would still have been difficult to increase the level of royal tribute demanded from the Kaveri region or the Tambraparni without replacing the ancient communal holders there, the *kaniyalar*, and thus attacking the religious privileges long vested with the riverine élite. To do this might have jeopardised the successful strategy of making the Vijayanagara lordship acceptable through their dharmic participation in temple affairs. And, of course, river-basin societies had military protection. In Tanjavur, a part of the large money wealth was deployed by the corporate landed élite to pay Vanniyar soldiers from north of the Kaveri and Kallar soldiers from the south to defend the delta from attacks; similarly, the Tambraparni valley was defended from predations by hiring Maravar soldiers as well as Telugu fighters, even though both were excluded from holding lands in the irrigated valley. It is true that the warrior folk protecting the river-basins of Tamil country gradually did encroach upon wet lands at the edges of the irrigated systems, but such encroachments added an interest for these warrior groups to defend and therefore raised the price of more central control by Vijayanagara and its successor regimes.

COMMUNITY AND EXPLOITATION

Among the differences between the riverine and dry-upland societies was the way that wealth was produced and labour was organised. Wealth in the irrigated zones of the peninsula was produced by the labour of a large agrestic servitude class and was realised, in large part, by the export of its rice surplus to Sri Lanka, northern Coromandel, and Malabar. While the internal bulking of rice surpluses seemed to have been in the hands of the landholding élite, foreign traders, as on other coasts of the peninsula, were the major Coromandel trade castes – Tamil Chettiyars and Telugu Komatis and Balijas as well as indigenous and foreign Muslims. The high level of wealth generated by reliable rice surpluses was produced by the labour of low-status cultivators who held little or no land of their own. Control of this labour force was as important as adequate water for cultivation for the wealth produced in places like the Kaveri and Tambraparni valleys; the *kani* right pertained especially to water and labour. Maintenance of existing irrigation works and drainage systems and their regular extension to new lands was no more the responsibility of a central state in the sixteenth century than it was in previous centuries. Communal holders of the Kani right deployed part of their labour control to maintain anicuts and other irrigation works, and they collectively supervised the distribution of water among fellow *kani*-holders. Temple lands in the river valleys were similarly managed and enriched as an extension of the high-caste élite landholding in any locality.

However, all in the Tamil wet zone depended upon the labour of despised and untouchable Pallas and Pariyans. The formation and maintenance of this workforce was as vital to wet-zone agriculture as water itself, but little is known of the ways in which this force of low workers were bent to their exploitation. In the absence of a state policing capability to support agrestic servitude, the most plausible explanation for the continued expansion of the riverine workforce is that people from the adjacent uplands and dry plains were willing to exchange their hazardous independence in this turbulent age for the secure food and shelter offered by labour in the wet fields of the Brahman and Vellalar élite of Tanjavur and Tirunelveli and the Kamma and Reddi landed élite the Krishna-Godavari delta. Submission for survival made for a tractable lower stratum in these river valleys, one that did not threaten the élite management there nor combined to challenge outside oppressors as the people in neighbouring Tiruchirappalli did in 1429.

Tiruchirappalli was one of the intermediate, mixed-cropping

zones between the riverine basins with social hierarchies dominated by communally organised élites of Brahmans and Vellalars, and the clan-organised, more egalitarian societies of the dry zones of the peninsula. In mixed-cropping zones – including the greater part of the Vijayanagara heartland – the potential for reliable irrigation was lower than in the river valleys and was achieved by tank reservoirs and wells. Here, high-status cultivating groups, who eschewed the plough in imitation of Brahmans in riverine areas, cultivated both wet and dry fields. Such mixed zones of wet and dry cropping comprised substantial parts of Madurai, Arcot, and Kongu in the Tamil plain, the Karnataka *maidan* and some parts of Rayalaseema and Telangana.

Mixed- and dry-cropping zones contributed such major commodities as cotton and indigo to the peninsular economy; they were not merely backward versions of riverine economies. Beginning in Chola times, such areas, along with coastal ports, comprised scattered centres of high commerce and were major corridors of trade. During the Vijayanagara period the pace of commercialisation had quickened led by two factors: overseas trade and the deliberate policy of territorial magnates of augmenting their money revenues through customs fees. In upland Kongu, modern Coimbatore, and Salem, in the low southern plain of modern Pudukkottai and Ramnad, and in the northern Tamil and Andhra dry plains of Tondaimandalam and Rayalaseema, were numerous trade centres where commercial groups gathered and which they controlled through a head merchant, where they supported temples, and where commodities from all over the dry- and mixed-cropped areas were assembled for shipment, usually by bullock trains, to markets near and far. The commodities that made up this trade were textiles, cotton, indigo, garden crops, oil seeds, millets, and palm and fruit products. Bullocks used in long and short transport and in cultivation everywhere were reared in these mixed and dry zones which afforded the required pasturage. Moreover, here, more than in the wet zones, temples provided the vital centring to all local communities which in the wet areas was achieved by élite communities of ancient corporate privilege with heavily inscribed religious sanctions.

'Community' in Indian sociological and popular usage means

'caste', a concept so englobing and essentialising as to displace all others. The more general meaning of 'community' – a people living in the same place and sharing many values – has all but disappeared and with that the possibility of defining local affinities in terms other than the ranking of social groups in accordance with normative principles that might have little to do with how actual local societies were, or are, constituted. Caste was surely one of the principles of social organisation in sixteenth-century South India, but there were other kinds of affinities that were more important. Certainly, political and religious affiliations and their interrelationship during Vijayanagara times was of the first importance if on no other basis than the evidence of that time speaks much more about chieftaincy and sect than about caste. But it is necessary to admit that not much is known about the religious component of local identities then, however more is known about that than the usual preferred explainer of most Indian social phenomena – caste.

RELIGION, SOCIETY, AND IDEOLOGY

Aggregative assessments of temples in the Vijayanagara kingdom – the number of temples, their distribution, their sectarian affiliations – are few, and the same is true (if anything, our ignorance is the more profound) about religious networks centred on the sectarian organisation (*matha*, 'seminary' or 'monastery') of the age.

The leader of a sectarian centre, *mathadipati*, was among the most powerful men of the Vijayanagara age. Many enjoyed royal patronage and confidence that resulted from serving as the spiritual adviser (*rajaguru*) of kings and great chiefs of the realm. Saluva Narasimha's preceptor, Kandadai Ramanuja Ayyangar, was the head of the Tengalai Srivaishnava *matha* at Tirupati, and as a result of Narasimha's support, this Brahman held affairs of the Tirupati temple in his grip during the late fifteenth century. Similar influence over the affairs of the Ahobalam temple was exerted by the head of the Vadagalai Srivaishnava *matha* there who served as the guru of the powerful Nandyala chief. Krishnadevaraya's preceptor was the head of the Madhva *matha* at Tirupati.

Unlike other religious personages of the time, the head of a *matha* was not limited by collegial relations with other priests. All property donated to a *matha* to support instruction of neophytes and sectarian propaganda was the personal wealth of the head, who determined those to be initiated and who was to be appointed his successor. A head of a *matha* was usually a Brahman except in the case of Virasaiva's whose non-Brahman heads enjoyed the same high standing among devotees and others. The *mathadipati* toured the areas where his followers lived, and his progress was conducted in the manner of a king, on elephants, with the royal paraphernalia of umbrellas and drummers, and with large retinues. And like the Vijayanagara rayas, these heads sent their agents to where their followers lived to advise them in matters spiritual and secular, to collect funds for the order, sometimes to initiate new members, to arbitrate disputes among them, and to preach the doctrines of the sect. Among the most vigorous and successful of such itinerant propagandists were those attached to the Srivaishnava *matha* at Tirupati and at Ahobalam and the *karayakarta* and *mudrakarta* attached to the Virasaiva *matha* at Srisailam.

At the opposite pole of political authority from kings and great chiefs and their preceptors was the world of local chiefs whose relations with local temples, sects, and cultural traditions were as important. We are afforded an excellent insight into this by Roghair's study of 'The Epic of Palnad' or 'the story of the Palnad heroes': *palnati virula katha*. In this remote, western corner of Guntur, the struggle between local Velama cultivators, under their epic chief, Brahma Nayudu, and their Haihaya Raju overlords has been recited and re-enacted for possibly eight centuries. At another level, the struggle was also between the 'indigenous' Vaishnavism of the Velamas and the 'foreign' Virasaivism of their opponents. This story (*katha*) was probably committed to written Telugu in the early fifteenth century at about the same time that inscriptions were engraved on two of the temples of Karempudi where the epic is centred and where Brahma Nayudu and the heroes of the epic are worshipped. Inscriptions of Karempudi continue to refer to the 'heroes' until as late as 1625, and during the present century, the Siva 'temple of heroes' has been the seat of Brahman preceptors of the Velama cultivators and others who worshipped there.

Temples and *matha* were prime instruments for Vijayanagara political purposes; they enjoyed a moral standing which no Hindu kingdom could ignore or oppose. Every temple can be said to have represented, or to have constituted, as a single entity the diverse peoples whose worship it attracted. While it is true that major Hindu institutions were increasingly to be found in urban situations, sixteenth-century South India was still rural, and older communal agrarian rights, which remained intact, were registered in, as well as protected by temples. In villages and localities there were often the shrines of guardian deities – usually goddesses – whom all of the place worshipped; there were also lineage shrines sheltering the tutelaries of dominant landed folk as well as the shrines of deities who protected the people and welfare of larger territories. These territorial guardian temples existed before Vijayanagara and were dedicated to some manifestation of Siva in Tamil country as in Telangana.

Gods selected as well as protected their worshippers, which lent temples their social significance during the fifteenth and sixteenth centuries and made them prizes for Vijayanagara to win over. Temple worship involved the complex transactions of a body of worshippers and the god of their devotion; there was selection of who could offer worship and who could receive the fruits of worship. The last were usually transvalued substances such as food offered for the sustenance of the god or clothes for his or her adornment; these were returned to devotees as *prasadam*, the god's grace. Eligibility to give to and to receive from a god, and the order in which giving and receiving occurred, was monitored by priests and devotees, for such transactions defined an entire community and the ranking of persons and groups within it. Accordingly, the lowest social groups were excluded from worship, adding to their isolation and degradation. Failure to assure that only those fit to worship participated, and in the correct order, could discredit and shame a deity and its devotees.

The ease with which the remote sovereignty of the rayas came to be exercised over the Tamils and others depended upon the favour they showed to Tamil deities; but it depended, too, upon the same sort of favour to most local magnates in their undisturbed mastery of the countryside and many of the new towns. Chiefs, for their part, used their connections with the largely ritual Vijayanagara kingship to enhance their authority on their own turfs. Thus the great foreign sovereigns of Vijayanagara added to the greatness of the little kings of Tamil country and elsewhere. This was *dayada* of the *Ajnapatra*, the sharing of sovereignty between great kings and territorial chiefs.

The latter were principal movers in the integration of religious affiliations in which often humble lineage and clan shrines under their protection mimicked the grandeur of canonical temples. But more was done than this. Such new shrines 'explained' themselves and their status in new texts. Temple chronicles of the sixteenth and seventeenth centuries – *mahamatya* and *sthalapurana* – provided myths about two sorts of connection: that between a particular people and their guardian deity – most often a goddess – and that between the latter and older territorial gods of the great pantheon, usually Siva. Tamil poems of praise – *satakam* – of the same period added to these ideological constructions. In the process, chieftainship and the standing of the dominant landed people represented by chiefs were enhanced by the binding of local guardian spirits to more distant and majestic divinities. This was but an extension at the level of religion of what had been happening in secular politics to bring local magnates and superior lordships of the Vijayanagara age into closer relationship. Political integration of the age was thus matched, especially in the extensive agricultural and political frontier, by a linking of local magnates, their penates and ancient canonical gods. That would seem to be the evidence of Tamil country at least.

Enhanced and more integrated secular and divine lordships in Tamil country and elsewhere closed some of the distance between Vijayanagara kings and the multitude of chiefs of the peninsula. But, at the same time, this amalgamation of secular and divine lordship, by strengthening territorial bonds and resistance to external coercion, limited the centralising forces emanating from sixteenth-century Vijayanagara. Most of the means at the disposal of Vijayanagara kings and their agents for extending central authority were also available to lesser magnates: better and more armed soldiers, larger money revenues, and closer administrative control from urban political and commercial centres. There seems to have been no lag between the adoption of stronger, centralised control of people and resources by the Vijayanagara ruler and by 'subordinate chiefs' whom Krishnadevaraya was purportedly instructed by his ministers to overawe according to the *Rayavachakamu*. Both were strengthened simultaneously, and one consequence of this was the increased exploitation of lower orders of the society by both local and central authorities; another consequence was an era of military adventurism by Vijayanagara against the Muslim regimes to the north as a means of expanding the prizes of lordship in the peninsula. This second consequence will be dealt with in the next chapter.

South Indian communities were not single, undifferentiated moral entities in the sense that caste implies. Dominant landed communities were internally differentiated. All major landed groups in South India were territorially subdivided into local segments which in places like Kongu acted as clans, possessing their own chiefs and guardian deities within which interactions and loyalties were the most enduring. Marriage arrangements also differentiated families in any subcaste or clan of landed folk. Within landed groups considerations of rank and standing entered into marriage alliances among families; these considerations were most exacting among chiefly families and more loosely graded with social distance from ruling lineages. Finally, wealth entered the calculus of marriage alliances within all landed groups, for marriage was one of several strategies for increasing the land held by a family.

It is also probable that the definition of 'lower orders' had undergone many changes by the sixteenth century. During the thirteenth century the southern peninsula began to undergo an urbanisation driven by the development of larger temples and chiefly fortifications. With their large priestly and non-priestly staffs and their ever-increasing throngs of pilgrims, temple centres fostered elaborate urban facilities and attracted permanent commercial and artisanal populations. Religiously-inspired urbanisation was soon augmented by political factors as chiefdoms and kingdoms became ever larger, better fortified and competitive. It was this which led to the demise of the Cholas and Hoysalas in their turn, especially when Muslim soldiers raised the whole level of military activity and violence. All of this had created the conditions for the rise of the Vijayanagara.

By the sixteenth century, the forces tending toward greater urbanisation were crowned by the cumulative impact of Vijayana-

POLITICAL ECONOMY AND SOCIETY

gara rule. Agents of the Rayas were urban magnates; their fortified headquarters were garrisons that underpinned dispersed Vijayanagara authority, and large bodies of soldiers and numerous chiefly courts made towns centres of wealth and consumption. Such political centres either were temple centres at the outset or they became that as a result of the largesse of chiefs. In these numerous new towns of the Vijayanagara period a major redefinition of 'lower orders' occurred, this having to do with the division of right and left castes.

In myth and in social process, the left division of castes in the Vijayanagara domains suffered the historical disadvantage of being marginal to the dominant rural-centred society in which they lived. The core of the left division in most places consisted of highly skilled artisan-trading groups and regional merchant groups; to this core was added a substantial section of untouchable producers of commodities such as the widely-traded leather commodities of Tamil and Telugu scavengers and leather workers (Chakkilars and Madigas). Additionally, in Tamil country, the left division included the large cultivating group of Pallis. This was anomalous since most important cultivating groups – Tamil Vellalars, Karnatak Vokkaligas, and Telugu Reddis – were either affiliated with the right division or were regarded with Brahmans and some transregional merchants and bankers (such as Telugu Komatis) as neutral or unaligned. The Palli affiliation to the left may be explained by their late emergence as dominant landholding cultivators and by their claim to a prior martial history and Kshatriya status. To the core of cultivators of the right division were added other agrarian groups such as most herdsmen, grain traders and transporters, those providing goods and services for village people, such as potters, barbers, washermen, non-Brahman priests, and untouchable field labourers (Tamil Paraiyans, Karnatak Holeyas, and Telugu Malas).

Differences between the interests of these two broad coalitions of agrarian and non-agrarian groupings certainly resulted in conflicts, and the pre-Vijayanagara historical record contains many examples of that. However, there is as much evidence of co-operation in support of temples and against outside oppressors as occurred at the fringes of the Kaveri delta in 1429–30 against the demands of Vijayanagara agents and their Tamil allies.

The pace of urbanisation during the fifteenth and sixteenth centuries altered the balance between the right and left coalitions of castes. Leading groups of the right division, whose core interests were agrarian, had become deeply implicated in town life and in the more generalised exchange systems of the age. At the same time, the left division of castes, the core of whose interests were commodity production for extended exchange, and whose locus of operations were the new towns of the southern peninsula, were in a better position to demand quality of status and social privileges with those of the right division. From the time of Devaraya I to Achyutadevaraya, inscriptions are found in many parts of the southern peninsula entitling right and left castes to the same privileges, including the privilege of holding processions and displaying emblems. Royal adjudications were sought and gained by the leading groups of left castes, skilled artisan-traders called Kanmalars among Tamils, Panchala in Karnataka, and Panchanulu in Andhra.

The increasingly congruent interests of leaders of the right and left coalition and the readiness of state-level officials to certify demands for equality of social standing by left castes were important changes. Now, equalising privileges that marked status could be achieved without resort to the violent conflicts that sometimes erupted before, and this diminished the needs for internal solidarity of both coalitions. There seems little reason to doubt, and some evidence to support, the proposition that heightened demands for money revenues through the entire chain of lordships in the sixteenth century were passed by the more powerful to the less powerful in the chain of production from which all wealth came.

FIVE

IMPERIAL COLLAPSE AND AFTERMATH: 1542–1700

The Vijayanagara kingdom at its greatest moment during the first half of the sixteenth century consisted of few durable elements. Though between 1509 and 1565 Krishnadevaraya, Achyutadevaraya, and Aliya Rama Raja proved competent warriors and statesmen, all were aware of the dangers of assassination by kinsmen and usurpation by other powerful families. By the sixteenth century both threats had been realised too many times for any ruler to be secure. Another hazard were the shifting alliances among the great warlord families of the kingdom. This was especially the condition in the Karnataka and Rayalaseema heartland, the base of royal authority during most reigns. Any king's power depended upon a coalition whose focus he was; a personal relationship with the king opened wide possibilities for any great Deccan magnate. Often a personal relationship could be strengthened by marriage of a daughter into the royal lineage. The powerful Rama Raja, titled *aliya*, 'son-in-law', claimed the throne as husband of the daughter of Krishnadevaraya, and though he was long frustrated in that ambition, some of his considerable authority later derived as much from this affinal connection as from being the son and successor of Aravidi Bukka. Combinations amongst powerful families were shifting and complex; all were alert to advantages and ready to seize political initiatives when the powers of a neighbouring chief or the king weakened.

Adding to this competitive and dangerous world of the great households of the kingdom was the Muslim factor. Throughout Vijayanagara history Muslim warriors played a part of coalition building. This began in pre-Vijayanagara times when Ala-ud-din Khalji's trusted commander Malik Kafur, a converted Hindu, was invited into the succession struggles between Pandyan princes and laid the foundation for the short-lived sultanate regime there. Though the Vijayanagara kingdom itself was launched with an ostensibly anti-Muslim ideology, in less than a century Muslim fighters served as commanders in Devaraya II's army. A prospective ally was not rejected for being Muslim by a Hindu magnate, nor a Hindu by a Muslim either in the Muslim Golconda or Hindu Vijayanagara.

Beneath the world of aristocratic coalitions and counter-coalitions was the no less politically contentious world of chiefs and their constituencies. These were based upon communal institutions of kinship, locality, occupational/caste affiliations in the right and left divisions, and upon sect and temple. While much of this communally based world of localities had been altered by the sixteenth century – partly the result of the character and structure of Vijayanagara power with its intrusive military outsiders and partly as the result of the forces of commercialisation and urbanisation – local sodalities in the southern peninsula retained a large capacity to frustrate the ambitions of the mighty.

For most historians, the kingdom was what Nilakanta Sastri called a 'war state', one ruled by warrior-chiefs whose whole being was bent on attaining ever greater military force to be applied to any enemy, Hindu and Muslim. The large and expanding frontier of the kingdom, it must be remembered, had long been to the Hindu South, not the Muslim-ruled North; the fruits of military success – in wealth, territory, and sovereignty – were principally garnered in Tamil country. Vijayanagara was also an incorporative regime, one that sought to win to itself the allegiance and military capability of the many warriors throughout the peninsula. These objects of Vijayanagara courtship were also chiefs, or 'little kings' – with armed men, horses, and firearms at their disposal and hence worth the wooing. And furthermore, Vijayanagara was a parasitic regime that extracted tribute from the productivity and commerce of its peoples and contributed little itself to either.

It is, of course, true that the Vijayanagara kings boosted the level of violence through its armies and the attendant privileging of its military agents to the greatest dignities and wealth available in the southern peninsula, but historians usually justify this by the heroic defence of Hinduism against Islam. Still, it is difficult to identify the ways in which Vijayanagara *as a state* made a difference. It is perhaps strange, and it may appear trivial, that one way in which Vijayana-gara influence may be seen to have mattered was in changes of architectural styles of temples.

EMBLEMATIC TEMPLES

As already observed, art and architectural historians speak of a 'Vijayanagara temple style' whose features distinguish it from all others. The researches of George Michell at Hampi and his comparative grasp of temples elsewhere in the peninsula leads him to observe that there was a sudden break in the style of temple construction in the fourteenth century. Temples in the Hoysala and Kakatiya styles of the previous two centuries virtually ceased to be built, and, for a time during the fourteenth century, a simpler and earlier Deccan style was reverted to for shrines built at Vijayanagara and elsewhere in its hinterland.

The very first datable shrines constructed at Hampi during the first dynasty of Vijayanagara were devoted to Jaina deities. This not only manifested the continued importance of that religion in Karnataka, and perhaps even the allegiance to it by the early Vijayanagara kings, like the earliest of the Hoysalas, but also suggests a deliberate symbolic shift from that of previous Hindu regimes whom Vijayanagara had succeeded. A style very like that of the ancient Chaluyan kingdom of Badami and its temple complexes at Aihole and Pattadakal seemed to be affected. The anachronistic Deccan style of temple found at Vijayanagara was imitated at the Saiva centre of Sringiri; for example, the Vidya Shankara temple of the mid-fourteenth century, associated with Vidyaranya, the Raja-guru of the founders, was built to a Deccan plan.

By the middle of the fifteenth century, when a distinctive Vijayanagara style of temple had begun to evolve, its core design was derived from Tamil-country and late Chola shrines. The Ramachan-dra temple was at the symbolic centre, the urban core of Vijayana-gara, where royal ceremonies were enacted; it was probably begun by Devaraya I in the early fourteenth century in imitation of late Chola temples. Other places where this southern temple style was found at about the same time was Penukonda, at temples dedicated to Siva and to Rama, and at Srisailam, another Saiva centre patron-ised by the Saivite kings of the first dynasty. A mature Vijayanagara style was only achieved in the time of Krishnadevaraya.

This style continued Chola forms, but certain Chola elements were raised to a previously unknown monumentality, especially the

gateway, or *gopuram*. The Virupaksha temple at Hampi, though its
foundations are ancient, was substantially rebuilt in Krishnadevaraya's time; similarly, the Vithala shrine, begun by Devaraya I, was
expanded at the time of Krishnadevaraya. Shortly after, other major
temples of Hampi were constructed to the same large scale as were
temples in such chiefly centres as Tadpatri and Lepakshi and at the
older temple centres of Ahobalam and Kalahasti. The mature
Vijayanagara style began to find its way back to its origins in Tamil
country with additions to the Ekambaranatha and Varadaraja
temples at Kanchipuram, the Nataraja temple at Chidambaram, the
Jalakanteshvara temple at Vellore, and at Srirangam and Tiruvannamalai. All came to be marked with the distinctive towering gateway
called 'Rayagopuram', and many also had portrait statues of Vijayanagara kings and other important patrons. Thus, personal iconographic connection was established between these most important
shrines and the great political figures of the time. The seventeenth-
century Nayaka kingdom temples of the peninsula steadfastly held
to this Vijayanagara style, displaying even more monumentality and
elaborating the motif of sculpted animal pillars introduced earlier.

Considering the symbolic power of temples in Vijayanagara
times, it is likely that these stylistic developments conveyed important meanings to contemporaries, as they do to the modern architectural historian. One meaning was that the Vijayanagara state was
of surpassing ritual importance for Tamil, Telugu, and Kannadiga
subjects of the rayas and their chiefs. Historians have insisted that
there was much more to the Vijayanagara state, of course, and one of
the chief foci of their arguments pertains to what is called 'the
foreign policy' of the kingdom during the last several decades of its
greatness. One reason for attention to this policy is that its failures
served to explain why the great kingdom collapsed, leaving the way
open for Islam to resume its march southward in the seventeenth
century. If not the result of the bold, if perhaps misconceived
foreign policy of Aliya Rama Raja in the middle decades of the
sixteenth century, why should this powerful kingdom have so
suddenly and catastrophically crashed? Such a question does not
parody the conventional historiography on Vijayanagara, but it
does draw attention to the false robustness attributed by most
historians to the kingdom and their unwillingness to apprehend the

many limits upon Vijayanagara power and authority even in its heyday.

RAMA RAJA'S RISE AND DIPLOMACY

None probed these limits so completely or so ruthlessly as Rama Raja, son-in-law of Krishnadevaraya, contender against the latter's chosen successor, Achyutadevaraya, and the most powerful Vijayanagara lord of the mid-sixteenth century.

His father, Aravidi Bukka, was a major player in the dangerous game of usurpation at the time of Saluva Narasimha. Even more dangerously, Aravidu Bukka shifted his loyalty to the rising Tuluva nayakas before they snatched the throne from Saluva Narasimha's son. With what in other times might have been deemed sedition, Rama Raja appears to have served for a time as commander in the army of the Golkonda sultanate as other Rayalaseema chiefs did and were to do again. Then, with his father, he shifted allegiance to the Tuluvas and served Krishnadevaraya at the same lofty rank as his father. As a commander of the Raya's army he distinguished himself against the Orissan Gajapati and also in campaigns against Bijapur and Golkonda. Having married into the royal family as well as being widely regarded as a suitable candidate for the throne, Rama Raja was supported by a broad coalition of magnates to succeed in preference to the two brothers of Krishnadevaraya, Tirumala and Achyutadevaraya. The latter was designated as his successor just before Krishnadevaraya died, and at the same time Rama Raja was appointed his chief minister. When Krishnadevaraya died in 1529, the powerful coalition backing Rama Raja, including many of his kinsmen, challenged the late king's decision and openly supported Rama Raja's enthronement.

Twice thwarted, it is hardly surprising that when Achyutadevaraya died in 1542 Rama Raja should again have been pressing against the royal gates of Vijayanagara nor that by then he should have been successful. But this success required raising the military stakes even higher to overcome his opponents. Unhesitatingly he did this by entering into an agreement with the sultan of Bijapur. The latter was to join in the struggle against the still powerful allies of Achyutadevaraya, the Salakarajus, who now supported the candidacy of their

kinsman Tirumalaraya against Rama Raja's candidate, and Achyutadevaraya's nephew Sadasivaraya. Several fierce battles were fought
between the two coalitions – at Gandikota, Penukonda, Kurnool,
and Adoni – before success came to Rama Raja, and this was only
after his ally Ibrhahim Adil Shahi entered the fray. In 1543 the
adolescent Sadasivaraya was crowned and Rama Raja was declared
his regent.

To the older nucleus of the regent's power, consisting of the
powerful chiefs who had followed his father, were added his two
seasoned warrior brothers, Venkatadri and Tirumala, and his own
five sons and other kinsmen. All were given high posts as governors,
often replacing Brahman officers; this fortified the coalition of
chiefs on whom Rama Raja had long depended and who provided
the troops and their commanders for his strong rule over the great
peninsular territory that acknowledged the sovereignty of the
youthful Sadasivaraya. When that unfortunate boy attained his
majority in 1550, he was deposed, possibly imprisoned, and Rama
Raja began to rule in his own name.

Even before this, however, Rama Raja had launched new imperial
initiatives on two fronts. Early in his regency, he sought a more
secure imperial presence in the far south where nayaka control over
Madurai was being consolidated. Rama Raja's aim was not to abort
the latter development, but to check growing Portuguese influence
along both rich trade coasts at the southern tip of the peninsula. To
frustrate this, in 1544 he dispatched a large army under his nephew
Vithala to punish the Travancore raja Unni Varma for encouraging
Portuguese encroachments and for refusing to transmit a portion of
the trade tribute gained from the Portuguese to Vijayanagara.
Vithala was assisted in the campaign by Visvanatha and his son
Krishnappa, the nayaka rulers of Madurai, and the successful
progress of the campaign against the Portuguese and the Travancore
raja can be traced in inscriptions of the time as well as from Jesuit
records of Unni Varma's Portuguese ally. As a preliminary to this
campaign, Rama Raja had taken the precaution of proclaiming direct
rule over Tirunelveli, thereby denying it to either Madurai or to
Tranvancore, both of which regimes sought control of the central
Tambraparni basin. After victories on the west coast, Vithala led his
army across the peninsula, seizing the port of Tuticorin; he

remained in the far south for a decade longer in order to forestall a renewal of Portuguese penetrations on the Coromandel coast. That Vithala made Tiruchirapalli, rather than Madurai, his headquarters during these years suggests that neither he nor his mentor Rama Raja were much concerned about the ambitions of the Madurai nayakas. No efforts were made to deflect the consolidation of their authority suggesting that such a large and independent authority in distant Tamil country was not seen as a threat to or departure from the political arrangements thought proper and desirable under Vijayanagara.

The second front on which Rama Raja sought to establish greater imperial control was north of Vijayanagara. Here the game was more dangerous and, in the end, disastrous for the Rayas.

From the beginning, Vijayanagara kings had looked to northern Karnataka as a potential zone of authority; in this sense, as well as in their early temple building, theirs was a Karnatak kingdom. Vijayanagara inscriptions are found in northern Karnataka and in southern Maharashtra until the fifteenth century. However, the early Bahmani sultans Muhammed I and Mujahid (c. 1358–78) waged such successful wars for this territory that during the fifteenth century the Tungabhadra became a boundary between the two kingdoms, with the interfluvial tract of Raichur constituting a buffer that changed hands frequently. Krishnadevaraya's early sixteenth-century campaigns put Raichur in Vijayanagara hands for a time and provided a base from which Rama Raja launched his more aggressive northern campaign.

A combination of high skill and arrogance characterised Rama Raja's policies toward the Muslim sultanates of the Deccan in the judgements of most historians. The skill of his diplomacy produced an extended period – over a decade – of Vijayanagara hegemony in northern Karnataka, opening a new frontier of opportunity for warrior chiefs devoted to his interests. However, that balance of power hegemony sowed seeds of the bitter fruit of 1565 when the great city was humiliated and destroyed.

The five sultanate regimes that partitioned the Bahmani Deccan territory around the beginning of the fifteenth century were given an unforgettable infancy at the hands of Krishnadevaraya. The Nizam Shahis of Ahmednagar, the Imad Shahis of Berar, the Barid

Shahis of Bidar, and the Adil Shahis of Bijapur began ruling about 1490; the Golkonda regime of the Qutb Shahis came two decades later. Each struggled to replace Bahmani authority and resume the southward march of Islam in the peninsula; but each also struggled against internal enemies. This not only delayed the resumption of southern expansion to the verdant river valleys to the south, with the prospects of wealth unknown in the dry upland of the Deccan, but regularly threatened the existence of each regime. Krishnadeva-raya proved the implacable barrier to the realisation of their dreams of expansion southward after he smashed their alliance against him in 1510. That victory also won Raichur back and the possibilities of deeper penetrations by Vijayanagara into northern Karnataka and southern Marathi country.

When Krishnadevaraya died and the turmoil of Achyutadeva-raya's succession and Chellappa's rebellion still raged, the Deccan sultans struck back. Quili Qutb Shah successfully attacked the fortress of Kondavidu in 1530, but was forced to abandon it by Achyutadevaraya's vigorous counter-attack led by his governor of the eastern rajya, Salakaraju Tirumalayadeva, acting with the powerful local chief of the Velugoti family which dominated the Venkatagiri area from the thirteenth century. While Achyutadeva-raya was thus engaged on his north-east frontier and soon after with Rama Raja's attempted coup and Chellappa's rebellion in the south, Ismail Adil Shah of Bijapur seized the Vijayanagara forts at Raichur and Mudkal acting in concert with Amir Barid of Bidar. The two allies fell out soon after and therefore relieved Achyutadevaraya of the threat poised against the city itself. Shortly thereafter, more breathing-space was created by the death of Ismail Adil Shah in 1534 and a succession struggle there. To add to these convoluted politics, one of the candidates in the Bijapur succession struggle, Asad Khan of Belgaum, on the border of northern Karnataka and southern Maharashtra, entered into an agreement with Achyutadevaraya and the Portuguese to support his candidacy for the Bijapur throne. Achyutadevaraya duly invaded Raichur both to regain his territory and simultaneously to defeat enemies of Asad Khan. A recon-ciliation between the new Bijapur sultan and Asad Khan ended the possibility for Achyutadevaraya to achieve more than this restoration of Raichur. There matters stood when Achyutadevaraya died in

1542 and Rama Raja became the virtual ruler of Vijayanagara as regent.

The momentary dissaffection of Asad Khan exposes a deeper characteristic of politics of the era, whether among Muslims or Hindus. That was the constant grasping about by great and small lords of the Deccan for advantage through coalitions and alliances, a strategy which recognised no frontiers between the Hindu kingdom and its supposed Muslim adversaries to the north. Contemporary Muslim chronicles and accounts later gathered by Colin Mackenzie document such activity and its consequences in the grand alliance of sultans formed against Rama Raja's Vijayanagara and, after his defeat in 1565, the cynical and violent efforts that were made by Vijayanagara grandees to put themselves into the same regency role as that held by Rama Raja, that is as the greatest generalissimo of South India.

One set of complicated diplomatics began in 1543 or 1544, just as Rama Raja, as regent, took direction of the kingdom. The sultan of Ahmadnagar, Burhan Khan (reign 1509–53), and Ibrahim Adil Shah of Bijapur agreed that Ahmadnagar would invade and seize territory from his enemy the sultan of Bidar while Ibrahim would invade Vijayanagara. Each thus sought to assure that the other ally would not be free to seize their lands while they were engaged in plundering other neighbours. Rama Raja foiled this, cleverly, by a stunning long-distance strike against Ahmednagar where he managed to capture Burhan Khan. The latter was easily persuaded to ally himself with Rama Raja and with the new sultan of Golkonda, Jamshid (reign 1543–50), for an invasion of Bijapur. Ibrahim Adil Shah met this danger by entering into a separate peace with Rama Raja through the concession of territory; this freed him to deal with his less threatening Muslim enemies whom he defeated. In 1549, another intricate, machiavellian dance was begun with Bijapur, again, the chief prospective victim. This time the allies of Rama Raja held fast permitting him, with an army led by Sadasiva Nayaka of Ikkeri and by Burhan Khan, to defeat Ibrahim at Kalyani, the ancient Chalukyan capital.

Rama Raja added to his weapons against Muslim enemies by sheltering a Golkonda prince named Ibrahim from the wrath of his sultan father, and when the latter died, Rama Raja provided the young prince with 30,000 foot-soldiers and cavalry under his brother Venkatadri to take the throne of Golkonda. Having made these efforts to create an ally in Golkonda, Rama Raja decided to take up the cause of a now weakened Bijapur against Golkonda a few years later. This was not the first time that Rama Raja sought to arbitrate power there, as his arrangement with Asad Khan and the Portuguese some time before indicate.

However, in 1555, Rama Raja shifted his policy, and when his Golkonda protégé, Ibrahim, and the sultan of Ahmadnagar invaded Bijapur, he supported Bijapur, perhaps hoping thus to make it a client. Still later, Rama Raja struck again against his protégé the sultan of Golkonda, by unleashing close supporters in Rayalaseema to seize southern Golkonda territories for themselves. The chiefs of Kandbir, Rajamundry, and Venkatagiri took Golkonda forts and their adjoining territories at Kondapalli, Ellore, and Gandikota. The Vijayanagara regent tried to strike even closer to the heart of his erstwhile protégé by fomenting a conspiracy among the Telugu commanders of garrison troops (*nayakawari*) of forts in the centre of Golkonda; they agreed to hand their forts to Rama Raja's soldiers when the latter invaded Golkonda. This conspiracy was discovered by Ibrahim and thwarted by a large-scale massacre of Telugu garrison soldiers.

DENOUEMENT

For twenty years Rama Raja's daring and ruthless policy had worked well. Vijayanagara was seldom exposed to the dangers the city had known from the Bahmanis during the fifteenth century. To achieve all this, Rama Raja had to have a strike-force able to intervene in affairs north of Vijayanagara on short notice, and this was supplied by a set of chiefs in Karnataka and Rayalaseema willing to risk war for a portion of sultanate territory near their chiefdoms and the loot that came with seizing a sultanate city. Over the years, his men held major parts of Dharwar and Bankapur and many lesser places in Raichur and elsewhere, and many a chiefly temple must have been built with the pillage from Bijapur or Ahmadnagar. The main commanders of this force were his brothers – Tirumala and Venkatadri – and Sadasiva Nayaka of Ikkeri, his Marlborough. All had become expert in the use of artillery by then, even though their gunners were Portuguese or Muslim, just as the light horse- and foot-soldiers of the Muslim regimes were often Marathas. Moreover, Muslim chroniclers of the time were persuaded that Rama Raja's great advantage over any of his Muslim rivals was his treasury burgeoning from customs collected from the ports and towns of Vijayanagara. Such wealth both necessitated a reconciliation among the sultans and offered the prize of permanent possession of its sources.

Rama Raja's great game could not be played much longer, for he was now, in 1564, eighty. Anticipating the retribution that must come against Vijayanagara he had added to the defences of the city and other fortresses south of the Tungabhadra. He cannot have been surprised when the sultans agreed to end their long, divisive quarrels.

The initiative for this diplomatic revolution came from the most recent heavy losers in Rama Raja's game – Husain Nizam Shah of Ahmadnagar and Ibrahim Qutb Shah of Golkonda. The latter achieved the most difficult task of persuading Husain and Ali Adil Shah of Bijapur to give up their struggles in Maratha country and to seal their amity with a royal marriage. When Rama Raja learned of the grand alliance against him, he produced one of his own, calling upon dependent chiefs near and far, including the nayaka of Madurai, Krishnappa, who had recently succeeded his father Visvanatha. Krishnappa is said to have sent his able minister and chief agent of his consolidation of power in Madurai, Ariyanatha Mudaliar, with a large force to join Rama Raja as he marched northward to meet the assembled Muslim force on the Krishna River, eighty miles north of Vijayanagara. There, on the south bank of the river, in late January 1565, the Vijayanagara armies were at last decisively defeated, Rama Raja and many of his kinsmen and dependants were killed and the city opened to sacking by a combination of Golkonda soldiers and poligars from nearer to Vijayanagara.

Rama Raja's warrior brother Tirumala survived the battle and brought the remnants of the once great army to Vijayanagara. Soon after, at the approach of the celebrating Golkonda army, he sought a place of greater security. This may have been Penukonda, a long-time royal stronghold, 120 miles and eight days' journey south-east of Vijayanagara; others believe that Tirumala took refuge behind the high walls of Venkatesvara's temple at Tirupati, still further away. The Muslim confederates immediately retrieved most of the territory that had been seized by Rama Raja during the previous twenty years, but certain places remained in Hindu hands for a longer time: Adoni was held until 1568 and Dharwar and Bankapur until 1573. After looting and a brief occupation, Vijayanagara was left to a future of neglect which has only been lifted recently by archaeologists and art historians working at Hampi. Less than a year later, the sultanate confederates fell out. Bijapur attacked Ahmadnagar and Golkonda joined forces with the latter. Some contemporary accounts even relate how Tirumala was approached to become a co-belligerent against Bijapur in the resurgent struggles! This last scheme did not materialise, leaving Tirumala free to commence his rule of the kingdom, nominally as regent, for Sadasivaraya was still alive and remained so until perhaps 1575. Vijayanagara appears to have been reoccupied by Tirumala for a time after his victors departed, but his efforts to repopulate the city were frustrated by attacks upon it by Bijapur soldiers who might have been invited there by Peda Tirumala, Rama Raja's son, who opposed his uncle's seizure of the regency. Tirumala may also have decided to leave Vijayanagara because of the support that Peda Tirumala, his nephew, enjoyed there. In any case, he moved back to Penukonda where the court was to be.

THE KINGDOM DYING AND DIVIDED

Tirumala, a younger son of Aravidi Bukka, ruled as regent until 1572; his son, Sri Ranga, ruled as king as did his grandson, Venkata II, who succeeded in 1586, and Sri Ranga II, in 1614. In 1630, the royal line reverted to the descendants of Rama Raja through Peda Tirumala, with Venkata III and Sri Ranga III ruling until 1650. Thus did the Aravidu dynasty survive for a century the defeat of 1565 and the flight from Vijayanagara. For the most part these late kings were pathetic pawns in the struggles among the great Telugu houses either to seize and revive the Vijayanagara throne or to prevent others from doing so. Not surprisingly therefore, the later kings had to seek the goodwill, or self-interest, of sometime Muslim allies against other Hindu and Muslim foes. Neither proved reliable instruments for restoring the great kingdom, of which only a shell remained. Still, that was enough for some imperial grandees to fight two civil wars, while at the same time, others were establishing new kingdoms whose legitimacy derived from the 'Raya samasthanam'. The latter included the kingdoms of the nayakas of Karnataka and Tamil country and the hundreds of 'little kingdoms' of poligars and other smaller sovereignties.

The nayaka regimes appear to have come into existence around 1530, well before the defeat of Aliya Rama Raja's army on the Krishna River and the sacking of Vijayanagara. Though some historians haggle about when it is appropriate to speak of these purported Vijayanagara 'successors', there is general agreement that it might well have been around 1530. Given this agreement, there is a paradox that has never been faced, much less resolved, in Vijayanagara historiography. It is this: at the moment that the kingdom was at its greatest, during the reign of Krishnadevaraya, who died in 1529, 'successor' regimes existed, and the kingdom, or 'empire', was beginning to be partitioned into independent states consisting of some of its richest parts: Tanjavur, Madurai, Gingee, and Ikkeri. Obviously, this contradiction can itself be dissolved only by conceding that the Vijayanagara kingdom, at the moment when its central authority was greatest, was a weakly-centralised polity, one in which the most important of its parts were regarded by contemporaries as independent in every respect save that they could not claim to be fully-fledged kingdoms. This last condition was to be achieved not long after the time of Aliya Rama Raja. But even during a time of his vigorous authority, in the middle decades of the sixteenth century, we have seen that in relation to the Madurai nayakas, neither he nor his nephew, Vithala, attemped to alter the considerable independent power that was being consolidated at Madurai under its nayaka rulers. Presumably it was not deemed a breach of Vijayanagara royal authority for Visvanatha Nayaka and his son Krishnappa to exercise independence over a principality of over 36,000 square miles.

The crucial element of the history of the final century of Vijayanagara by successors of Rama Raja, descendants of Aravidi Bukka, was the struggle to reconsolidate a degree of central authority against powerful military overlords bent upon creating independent monarchies. All of this was set against relentless pressure from Bijapur and Golkonda. Both sultanates had, since their foundation a century before, become more effectively centralised regimes than Vijayanagara in the sense that both had arrived at stable, hegemonic superiority over local chieftains. Both now sought to extend their authority southward in order to enlarge the base from which wealth could be appropriated from agricultural production and internal commerce or from the rich trade emporia on both coasts of the peninsula. By the late seventeenth century, this aggrandising expansion had been turned to a desperate flight of these sultans from the encroaching Mughals who soon after ended the careers of both.

After the defeat of 1565, two events signalled the futility of reconstituting a single, powerful kingdom. One was a civil war that began in 1614 and lasted for a decade. This involved scions of the royal Aravidu family for control of a throne which now possessed neither a capital nor even a fixed territory. The war began with the death of Venkata II, a nephew of Rama Raja and second son of the king Tirumala. Venkata had ruled from 1586 to 1614; his designated successor, Sri Ranga, failed to win the support of many imperial grandees on grounds of his doubtful legitimacy and capabilities. Many also considered Sri Ranga too dependent upon Raghunatha, the Nayaka ruler of Tanjavur, who had links to the displaced Tuluva family through his father and founder of the Tanjavur nakayaship, Sevappa, a brother-in-law of Achyutadevaraya. Such a connection placed Raghunatha outside the charmed circle of kinsmen of Aravidi Bukka. High Telugu imperial families thus were divided between supporters of the new king, Sri Ranga, led by Yachama Nayudu, or Nayaka, of the Velugoti family of Venkatagiri in Nellore, and another faction of grandees who supported another doubtful son of Venkata II, Ramadeva. The latter faction was led by a brother of the favourite queen of Venkata named Jagga Raya whose family held sway in eastern Kurnool.

Jagga Raya seized the initiative in a ferocious manner by murdering Sri Ranga and his family, an act which apparently lost him enough supporters to cause his defeat in a battle against Yachama Nayaka in 1616. This was fought on the Kaveri, near Tiruchirapalli, possibly because of the alliances betweeen Telugu royal aspirants and their Tamil allies. Yachama had the support of the nayaka of Tanjavur whereas Jagga Raya had the support of the nayaka Madurai, Muttuvirappa, and the nayaka of Gingee, Krishnappa. The only gainers from this warfare, in which Jagga Raya died, were the nayaka of Tanjavur who acquired valuable territory from neighbouring Gingee and the nayakas (or rajas) of Mysore and Ikkeri, who, by remaining aloof from this struggle, were free to strengthen their respective holds over Karnataka. Finally, there was the sultan of Bijapur for whom the warfare and divisions among the most powerful Telugu warlords opened new southern tracts in western Kurnool to his conquests. Any possible recrudescence of a powerful Vijayanagara was thereafter sealed by another period of blood-letting among the great households of Vijayanagara.

This occurred after the turbulent reign of Ramadeva in 1630. Then, the latter's choice of successor was contested by another of Rama Raja's relatives, and for five years longer the great Telugu households fought each other with nayaka kings of Tamil country – Tanjavur, Madurai, and Gingee supporting one set of Telugu grandees and Chamaraja Wodeyar of Mysore, and at one point the Dutch, supporting another faction.

The nayakas of Ikkeri in northern Karnataka, who had played a vital role in Rama Raja's adventures in the Deccan, stayed out of these two wars. During the first, in 1614, Venkatappa Nayaka (reign 1586–1629) opportunistically extended his power over neighbouring chiefs, bringing the Ikkeri kingdom to its apogee, with control over all of the Kanara coast (Tulu rajya) and a great part of the adjacent upland (Male rajya). His successor Virabhadra Nayaka (reign 1629–45) had little choice about fishing the waters stirred by the second Vijayanagara succession war of the 1630s, for he was preoccupied with recalcitrant chiefs whose powers his father had sought to expunge, but who now strove to wrest back lost authority and lands. In addition, Virabhadra had to fend off a usurpation of his throne by a royal kinsman, Virappa Nayaka. During the course of this second epoch of wars, Ikkeri and other Karnatak lords also faced two invasions by Bijapur, just as Telugu and Tamil magnates faced a similar onslaught by Golkonda into the Coromandel plain.

Lethal, fratricidal warfare among the great households of Vijayanagara during the middle 1630s stemmed not only from the determination among the Tamil country nayakas to prevent the enthronement of a potentially strong Vijayanagara king, already present during the earlier civil war, but also another factor which inflected strategies of all who inherited Vijayanagara authority in the southern peninsula. This was the degree to which kinship had become the basis upon which all great households constituted and preserved their power and formed alliances.

Aliya Rama Raja appears responsible for this patrimonialism. At the outset of his direct rule of the kingdom in 1542, after Achyutadevaraya's death, he replaced the Brahman commanders of major fortresses of the Karnatak-Andhra heartland of the kingdom with his kinsmen; he permitted more autonomy to the Telugu warrior chiefs, upon whom his power depended, than they had in the reigns of Krishnadevaraya and Achyutadevaraya, when significant authority had been vested in the Brahman servants of the kings in Tamil country as well as in Andhra. These Brahmans were not ritual specialists, nor sectarian leaders, nor scholars, but men trained in scribal, accounting, and military skills. They had stood above the framework of kinship affinities and allegiances of territorial chieftaincies in the core of the kingdom. This made them particularly suitable administrative and military instruments for Krishnadevaraya's daunting task of establishing royal authority in those tracts which his brilliant military victories won for his new dynasty. There seems to have been a backlash of chiefly authority against the restrictions imposed by Krishnadevaraya, and this was nurtured and exploited by Rama Raja, whose formidable coalition of Telugu chiefs was united by marriage ties among each other and often with the ruling family itself. Rama Raja, it is recalled, was married to a sister of Krishnadevaraya, and the Salakaraju family, upon whom Achyutadevaraya depended for his throne and his life against the cabals of Rama Raja and the rebellion of Chellappa, also had marriage links with the ruling family.

Rama Raja's reversal of Krishnadevaraya's policies for creating a more centralised regime meant a return to the earliest days of the kingdom when the five brothers of Sangama ruled the parts independently, except now there was a strong focus of royal authority in Rama Raja. He placed all of the parts of the kingdom under his sons and gave the high command of his army to his two able brothers, Tirumala and Venkatadri. This was a family business and on a very large scale; it was also the beginning of patrimonial politics which were to thrive in the peninsula until the consolidation of British rule, in the late eighteenth century. As long as Rama Raja held hegemonic royal power, he was willing for distant great households like Madurai and Ikkeri to grow stronger in return for their contributions to his armies. Beneath the power of Rama Raja and his weaker and beleaguered successors, patrimonial relations came to dominate all others as the basis of rule, and patrimonial politics – the wars among the great households – prevented either resistance to the encroachments of the sultanate regimes or the first flutterings of intervention of Europeans in the great political games of the time.

During the middle of the sixteenth century, Bijapur followed the lead of Vijayanagara in concluding treaties with the Portuguese by offering trade concessions in return for an uninterrupted supply of war-horses and other trade goods; this reversed several decades of attempts by the Muslims to drive the Portuguese from the western coast. In 1639, during the second civil war among Vijayanagara grandees, the Portuguese were enlisted as military allies by the nayakas of Madurai while the Dutch Company sided with the raja of Ramnad in one phase of the war; at the same time, Venkatapappa Nayaka of Ikkeri reversed his predecessors' opposition to the Portuguese trade monopoly on the Kanara coast.

Patrimonialism and trade became the two historical motifs of this last phase of Vijayanagara. The first had become the essential condition of politics in the post-Rama Raja era owing, in part, to the latter's preference for (or obligation to follow) this sort of politics and, in part owing to the fading significance of a ruling family which had no territorial base of its own as its kings fled successively to Penukonda, Chandragiri, and Vellore. The beleaguered kings had become a burden to those magnates, like the raja of Mysore, who occasionally appeared to be committed to preserving a viable Vijayanagara kingship and who therefore supported one or another of the successors of Rama Raja.

The latter's twelve-year campaign for the throne after Krishnade-varaya's death meant successive additions to his coalition of chiefs and concessions to chiefly power. By the time he had secured the throne in 1542, Rama Raja was unable – even if he had wanted – to revive Krishnadevaraya's policy of limiting 'subordinate chiefs' from above through a system of royal forts and garrisons and from below by supporting the local ruling credentials of the many poligars who garrisoned royal forts and held small chiefdoms. The tiger of chiefly power that Rama Raja rode successfully threw off his weaker successors. Now, great and small chiefs could no longer base their regimes on service ties to great kings, for there were none. Bereft of personal ties with and service under great kings, 'subordinate chiefs' were left with little else but a reversion to an earlier form of ritual obedience to shadowy Vijayanagara kings, while relying concretely upon the unifying relations and idioms of kinship. Territorial magnates sought to reinforce the patrimonialism that was thrust upon them; they contrived ideological and institutional surrogates for that earlier provided by the Vijayanagara kings. A new form of kingship was evolving during the sixteenth and seventeenth centuries, one that took its principles from the late Vijayanagara era of Rama Raja rather than that of Krishnadevaraya.

THE LATE MONARCHY: INTERNATIONAL TRADE AND REVENUE

Before discussing these new forms of monarchy, it is necessary to return to the world of commerce that provided development and therefore made it possible in the form it took then. The recent doctoral thesis of Sanjay Subrahmanyam on trade and the regional economy of South India from 1550 to 1650 provides valuable new documentation on the relationship of overseas, coastal, and inland trade and permits a somewhat better assessment of the political economy of the late Vijayanagara era when great commerce and changing political forms went hand in hand.

What is known of the international trade of the peninsula – its major ports, traders, and commodities – is far greater than what is known about the coastal and inland trade upon which it depended. There were always two different sets of commodities: high-value pepper, ginger, sandal, and fine textiles, and low-value paddy, timber, and coir. These commodity sets were complementary since the international trade vessels plying from Pulicat or Masulipatam,

Cochin or Bhatkal depended on the coastal and inland trades for part of their cargoes and for provisioning while on shore. Therefore, when the international port of Pulicat declined after the sack of Vijayanagara, it did so slowly and continued to service established commercial networks of coasters and bullock trains from the interior. The supersession of Pulicat as the primary Coromandel port of Vijayanagara by Masulipatam, Golkonda's chief port, was hastened and encouraged by the direct interest of the Qutb Shahi sultans in trade and pilgrim passage as well as by the early interest of Portuguese and Dutch traders. Masulipatam's situation and the trade attracted by its large population of 100,000 by the end of the sixteenth century helped to make it the major Coromandel port until it was overtaken by Madras around 1680. To provision its large population, Masulipatam had to be supplied from often distant places. After 1570, supplies for the town came from coastal Orissa in an annual flotilla of some forty ships bearing rice and other grains, edible oils, and other food-stuffs and carrying back raw cotton, tobacco (introduced here and in Tirunelveli by the Portuguese at about the same time), iron, and crucible steel smelted in the Masulipatam hinterland of Telangana.

Frustratingly little new information is available on two other aspects of the trade systems of the time: who were the major Indian participants in the international and related trades and what were the fiscal demands upon these trades?

From Subrahmanyam we learn that coastal traders differed from those involved in overseas trading. On the south-west coast, long-distance traders were foreign Muslims (*paradesi*) whereas the coastal and local trade were in the hands of local Muslims, or Mapillas. On the Kanara coast to the north, Konkani-speaking Saraswat Brahmans were the most important coastal traders with minor roles for other Hindu and Jaina merchants, but overseas trade was dominated by Arabs, Jews, Armenians, and some Christian offsprings of Portuguese miscegenation. In northern Coromandel, most coastal and inland traders were Telugus – Balija Nayudus, Beri Chettis, and Komatis – and in southern Coromandel ports, indigenous Marakkayar Muslims were important.

Subrahmanyam called the most important of all Coromandel trader 'portfolio capitalists'. This was a recognition of their complex and overlapping interests: in overseas, coastal, and inland trade as well as tax-farming for Golkonda and other regimes and as 'head merchants' for the European companies. Two such merchants of the early seventeenth century were the Telugu Balija brothers Achyutappa and Chinnana who were at the apex of internal and external trades on their own accounts and served the Dutch as brokers and bankers. In addition to all that, they also held tax-farms under Golkonda, the rajas of Chandragiri (who were scions of the Vijayanagara royal family) and other local rulers. Not surprisingly, this family of merchants provide the best-documented information on the linkage between the great trades of the age and fiscal systems and demands of various Coromandel regimes.

By the early seventeenth century, when Achyutappa and Chinnana and their kinsmen strode the commercial stage, there was no single political regime over the peninsula that the Vijayanagara kings had once called their own. But, neither then, when a Vijayanagara king claimed the entire peninsula, nor later, did royal treasuries regularly benefit from customs receipts from expanding commerce. Subrahmanyam finds no basis on which to support the notions of some scholars that anything besides tribute payments from foreign traders was realised by Vijayanagara kings; he also, with good reason, denies propositions about 'forced commercialisation' as Vijayanagara state policy. The benefits of commerce and its profits were obvious to all who had participated in commodity production and exchange in the southern peninsula whether Indian or foreign.

A distinction less fully developed by Subrahmanyam and others pertains to the fiscal implications of there being two fundamental production zones in the peninsula. On the riverine plains and along the coasts there were established production and crafting centres which permitted lucrative revenue-farming contracts. Here were valuable and viable circuits of production and exchange into which profitable investment could be made from the revenues that tax-farmers contracted to collect on behalf of the powerful Golkonda or the weaker nayaka regimes of Gingee or Chandragiri. However, in the upland zone of dry and mixed cultivation, the same level of production and exchange did not exist; all there was too dispersed for 'portfolio capitalists' like Achyutappa to combine tax collecting, agricultural trading, irrigation investment, and long-distance shipping and banking into a single successful, profitable operation. This zonal distinction depends, of course, on seeing revenue-farming, as Subrahmanyam rightly does, playing a constructive economic role, not a parasitical or extortionate one. In the extensive dry upland where large mercantile capitals were more difficult to mobilise, the role of entrepreneurs was more modest and was taken by local big men and chiefs. It was they who set up markets (*pettai*) in towns and organised the weekly fairs (*sandai*) that attracted merchants and consumers; it was these local big men who provided inducements to weavers and other producers to settle and work in small towns and industrial villages; and it was they who derived the revenue benefits from such entrepreneurship.

It is important to appreciate that such mercantilist activities were essential to those who dominated the upland agrarian frontier of the Vijayanagara age. For them, land revenue was not, nor could it be, the sole source of money income required to meet military and other costs. Soldiers, especially foreign mercenaries, were paid in cash as were many indigenous fighters, but most local soldiers were given land on which very low revenue was demanded. Chikkadeveraya of Mysore followed the latter practice in the seventeenth century, which caused a widespread uprising of ordinary cultivators led by Virasaiva priests (Jangamas); that was bloodily suppressed and resulted in the flight of Virasaivas from southern Karnataka.

By 1800, when British records became available, the extent to which such concessionary arrangements of the land-tax to soldiers existed is documented in the old Vijayanagara heartland and elsewhere as historical landed privilege called by the Persian term *in'am*. In 1805, Thomas Munro reported that over half of the 3.3 million acres of cultivated land in the Ceded Districts of Madras was held under tenures that paid almost no land revenue, and this was after efforts by several Muslim regimes during the eighteenth century – Tipu sultan and the nizam of Hyderabad – to claw back alienated revenue for their own uses.

Such massive alienations of revenue lands as reported by Munro in the Ceded Districts of Madras were matched, if not exceeded, by the tax-free status of lands held by temples and other religious institutions throughout the southern peninsula. This must cast serious doubt upon the persistently expressed view of scholars that productive land constituted the sole or principal basis of public revenue in pre-colonial times. The best lands in the zone of dry and mixed cultivation were irrigated by tanks or wells; these were heritable holdings of various privileged groups: priestly families, headmen or accountant families, or they were held as the communal property of dominant cultivating families of a locality, on shares which were periodically reapportioned among families.

This meant that most regimes of the sixteenth and seventeenth centuries were dependent on taxes raised from trade and industrial production to meet their needs. The sixteenth-century findings from the town of Aluvakonda, discussed in the preceding chapter, supports such a proposition, for it was found there that a large portion of the money revenue upon land was granted by chiefs of that town and territory as income to temples, and the largest category of revenue payers were industrial producers and merchants.

The nayaka kingdoms established during the sixteenth century offer other examples of the same processes, though each was organised in different ways. Yet more striking examples of how cultivated lands, which allegedly supported state regimes, were actually alienated by their rulers come from among the last of regimes to be established under the auspices of Vijayanagara in Ramnad and Pudukkottai.

THE NAYAKA KINGDOMS

Vijayanagara historians designate as 'nayaka kingdoms' three in Tamil country and two in Karnataka: Madurai, Tanjavur, and Gingee and Ikkeri and Mysore. These regimes are distinguished from all others in the southern peninsula in being larger than others and in enjoying a special historical significance in the minds of modern scholars. Madurai under Tirumala Nayaka, 1623–59, and Ikkeri under Venkatappa Nayaka, 1586–1629, were as extensive as the heartland of the Vijayanagara kingdom under Krishnadevaraya. Tanjavur and Mysore were not so large, but both had been and were to be kingdoms in their own rights, the former with its Chola past and Maratha future, and Mysore with its future kings who patronised modern historical scholarship. The standing of Gingee appears to rest on a Tamil-language history prepared in 1803 by a descendant of the shepherd chief who founded and first fortified Gingee. Narayana Pillai was encouraged to compose his *Karnataka Rajakkal Savistara Charitram* by the first British collector of the Gingee region, William Macleod, a military colleague of Thomas Munro who was also assigned administrative tasks; Narayana Pillai's history became part of the corpus of Mackenzie documents.

These several regimes share another important attribute: they were not located in Andhra and therefore they were not centrally involved in the coalitions of Telugu grandees and chiefs who fought over control of the Vijayanagara throne during the seventeenth century. Still, all of the nayakas, except those of Ikkeri, took some part in the complex and violent machinations of would-be successors of Rama Raja, and like other participants in these dangerous politics, the nayakas sought to avert the re-emergence of a strong Vijayanagara king capable of reducing their authority and territorial ambitions.

Another attribute which the nayaka regimes are thought to share by many historians is that they were 'successor states' in the same sense that Avadh and Hyderabad were of the Mughals. But the nayaka kings were not successors of Vijayanagara; they emerged as independent polities at the very zenith of the Vijayanagara monarchy, during the early sixteenth century. However, although these regimes exhibited clear characteristics of Vijayanagara, they also differed in important ways from it and from each other according to political, economic and cultural features of the regions of their provenance. Apart from the cynical participation of some of them in the travails of the Vijayanagara kings after the 1565 defeat, these five kingdoms, like the Vijayanagara order from which they emerged, were all patrimonial, military regimes; they all found ways of trenching upon the wealth of commerce and commodity production without, however, achieving (or even seeking) direct control over their regional economies; and they all patronised local systems of religious affiliation and made themselves masters of religious institutions. How these tendencies were manifested in the several nayaka regimes of the sixteenth and seventeenth centuries was conditioned by particular and prior conditions found in each region; it was also important that the two Karnataka regimes were ruled by indigenous chiefly families, while those of Tamil country were ruled by Telugus.

Histories of the three Tamil kingdoms were published between forty and sixty years ago and all sought to soften the charge that these regimes contributed to the ignominious demise of the Vijayanagara kingdom. Generally, the attempt is to date the independent rule of each as late as possible and to claim that its nayaka rulers before that time were loyal 'governors' or 'feudatories' of the Vijayanagara kings. But the facts are obstinately otherwise for the most part. The Ikkeri regime began when Chaudappa founded his *samasthanam* at Keladi before 1500 (Ikkeri, six miles away, was made the seat of its rulers around 1560 and remained so until 1640 when Bijapur invasions forced the better defences at Bednur, 40 miles from Ikkeri). The last of the eighteen crowned rulers of Ikkeri was deposed by Haidar Ali Khan in 1763, ending a royal line which lasted 265 years. The Mysore kingdom was founded by a line of chiefs whose local authority dated from the same time and was fostered in the same way by military service to Vijayanagara; however, the rule of the Wodeyar rajas of Mysore extended into India's independent era. The kingdoms of Madurai, Tanjavur, and Gingee were established less than half a century later by sons of Vijayanagara military commanders proclaiming themselves kings and undergoing royal anointment (*pattabhisekha*).

Little is actually known about the coronation rituals of any of these kings. Probably, though, the Vijayanagara model was followed as it was at Madurai according to the Telugu *Rayavachakamu* composed there in the late sixteenth century. Reminiscent of Vijayanagara coronation rites were the important place of the royal tutelaries. Krishnadevaraya's evocation of the divinity of his family tutelary is described by Portuguese witnesses of the *mahanavami* festival at Vijayanagara, and Achyutadevaraya, who was thrice crowned, invoked the authority of his personal god, Venkatesvara, at Tirupati, the major territorial Siva at Kalahasti, and the Tuluva tutelary at Vijayanagara. Also conspicuous in these coronations was the participation of Brahman ministers of the king, as in the cases of Krishnadevaraya and his minister, Saluva Timma, in 1509, and later Ragunatha Nayaka of Tanjavur and his illustriously learned minister, Govinda Dikshita. However, when kings were made, as Sadasivaraya was by Rama Raja in 1542, it was the non-Brahman king-maker, Rama Raja, that played the conspicuous role. The frequent inscriptional and literary references to coronations and also to the practice of ruling kings installing their sons as heirs-apparent (*yuvaraja*) makes a nonsense of the pious reiteration of historians that the nayakas of the sixteenth and early seventeenth century were merely royal officials. For the people that they ruled and in the inscriptions that they caused to be engraved, they were kings, even though they acknowledged the superior kingship of the rayas.

A widespread, if not universal, royal ceremony which followed immediately upon the anointing of a maharaja of the Tuluva or Aravidu lines, or a raja in the nayaka realms, was common food-taking by the ruler and his closest kinsmen and supporters. This signified a kind of parity among the participants in the sense of being members of the same ruling lineage (Sanskrit: *varga*; Tamil: *varukkam*). This practice was followed in Madurai and helped to define a ruling order of princes (*kumara-varukkam*) in that kingdom during the reign of Visvanatha Nayaka, which began in 1529. Madurai's nayaka rulers appear in other ways to have been more imitative of Vijayanagara royal practice than other great households.

But in Madurai, there was more than mere imitation of the rayas, for the Telugu rulers there seemed to have reached back to a pre-Vijayanagara method for achieving political solidity. They resurrected a Kakatiya practice of symbolically associating territorial chieftains of that realm with its kings by the metaphoric use of the royal fortress to stand for the realm as a whole. Great chiefs were notionally made responsible for a bastion of that fortress and hence for the kingdom as a whole. The inventive Visvanatha Nayaka recovered another Kakatiya practice by devising a system of military dependencies during the sixteenth century. 'Palaiyam' means military encampment and the keepers of them, called *palaiyakkarar* in Tamil, were constituted as a formal system of authority consisting of seventy-two autonomous chiefs – Telugu and Tamil – who were conceived as a ruling set, each the protector of a bastion of the Madurai fort and thereby a member of Madurai's ruling estate, the *kumara-varukkam*. Evidence from no other great household of the sixteenth century quite suggests the degree of integration of kinship and military and chiefly authority that was achieved at Madurai. In Tanjavur at the time, there appear to have been neither palaiyams nor poligars, and in other nayaka realms the relations between raja or nayaka and subordinate chiefs was more openly conflictful.

Nayakas in Tanjavur and to a lesser degree in Gingee left the ancient landed élite of Brahmans and Vellalars dominant over the rich, irrigated cultivation systems in both places. The share of production which these nayaka regimes enjoyed was possibly not different from what it had been in Chola times, though it was received in money, not kind. However, the fiscal regimes of these nayaka kingdoms drew substantial wealth from the advanced commerce in rice and textiles of the sixteenth century, much of which was also in the hands of the Brahman and Vellalar élite. Similar indulgence was shown by the nayakas of Madurai to the same élite landholders in the Vagai and Tambraparni river valleys, but there is a difference of importance to be noted. In Madurai, there was a highly-organised military force sustained by the palaiyam system that gave protection to the wet zones of the kingdom as well as the rest of its territory. In Tanjavur, and possibly also in Gingee, military protection was provided by mercenaries, paid out of the rice and textile surpluses and advanced commerce of both coastal realms. The nayakas of Tanjavur and also of Gingee appear to have realised their major income from the farming of the fixed shares of production claimed by them to élite tax-farming contractors. The latter purchased the right to collect the revenue which was partly in rice and textiles; this was then sold by the local tax-farmers to regional merchants who carried the commodities by oxen-loads either to the coasts for export to Sri Lanka, Malabar, and South-East Asia or to other interior market centres in the peninsula. The money received by the rulers of Tanjavur and Gingee from contracting out revenue collections permitted the hiring of fighters from the neighbouring dry zones or from some coastal communities where European deserters and their mestizo offspring offered themselves for military service.

In Karnataka, the ruling Ikkeri and Mysore houses seem not to have discovered satisfactory ways of dealing with the independent chiefs of their realms. During the sixteenth and seventeenth centuries, both ruling houses fought to maintain their overlordships against minor chiefs, from the one side, and the invasions of Bijapuri soldiers – often with the connivance of chiefs – from the other. Little wonder, therefore, that both Karnataka kingdoms steered a careful course around most of the civil strife of the time. Exceptionally, the Wodeyar raja of Mysore, Kanthirava Narasa, invaded the northern Madurai tract of Dindigal around 1655 possibly as his solution to the problem of recalcitrant chiefs; for one way of minimising his predecessors' problems with local Kannadiga chiefs was to extend his tributary catchment southward into Dindigal and Kongu (modern Salem and Coimbatore). But that kind of solution to recalcitrance among Karnatak chiefs fetched dangers as great, for the Wodeyar raja's incursions were met by counter-invasions from Tirumala Nayaka of Madurai with an army that reportedly had 25,000 Maravar troops. Tirumala Nayaka was probably exacting more than vengeance, for he, too, sought more tractable zones of exploitation than those of his southern flank, Ramnad and Pudukkottai, where martial Maravars were local rulers. In these last two places are discovered what was perhaps the fullest realisation of the connection of patrimonial authority and trade in Ramnad and Pudukkottai.

The Maravar kingdom of Ramnad was inaugurated by the Madurai nayaka Muttu Krishnappa in the early years of the seventeenth century, an act of conventional Indian overlordship. Maravars were a people with a notoriety as fierce hunters and fighters as ancient as the Tamil Sangam poetry of about the third century. Later, they served as soldiers under Pandyan, Chola, and Vijayanagara kings. It is not surprising, therefore, that the Maravars should have had powerful chiefdoms in Ramnad, nor that under their fighting chiefs they should have spread into Tirunelveli and other southern places by the fourteenth century, finally finding service in the armies of the nayakas of Madurai. The Maravar homeland remained in Ramnad, however, and here a major chieftainship arose centred upon Ramesvaram, sacred in the Ramayana legend as the link between India and Sri Lanka.

From the fifteenth century, the temple at Ramesvaram, also called Sethu, was under the protection and patronage of the Maravar chiefs who assumed the title of Udaiyan Sethupatis ('chiefs who were the lords of Sethu'). Visvanatha Nayaka of Madurai conquered Ramnad in the middle of the sixteenth century, drawn, no doubt, by the rich trade there and its customs income. This deprived the Sethupati chiefs of their glorious responsibilities and honours; but later Madurai nayakas reinstalled them, and by 1606 another Udaiyan Sethupati was issuing inscriptions commemorating his gifts to the god Ramanatha at Ramesvaram and constructing new shrines there. Thus, all of the appropriate royal activities were followed by the newly-minted Maravar kings of Ramnad, but the basis of their power remained the ancient military organisation of Marava clansmen to which had recently been added money income from the trade of their coastal ports. Portuguese and Dutch traders paid well for the right to trade exclusively on this famous 'Fishery Coast' of Ramnad, and the Portuguese were not inhibited from converting the fisherfolk there, the Paravars, to Christianity. Proceeds from this tribute plus the customs collected from pilgrims and traders to and from Ramesvaram supported a substantial military force whose core consisted of Maravar clansmen, organised under Maravar chiefs with ties of ritual and service to the royal Maravar Sethupati.

Kallars in Pudukkottai developed a similar type of organisation, and thanks to the recent ethnohistorical account of Nicholas Dirks, we are able to examine in greater detail how the military power of the Tondaiman rajas of Pudukkottai was sustained.

This was a small principality of 1,000 square miles lodged between the nayaka kings of Tanjavur and Madurai. It had been settled by field agriculturists during Chola times when the tract constituted a buffer between the Chola kingdom and the Pandyas; it was also a major trade corridor connecting ports at the southeastern tip of the peninsula with Chola and Pandya countries as well as with the major transpeninsular trade routes linked to Malabar ports on the Arabian Sea.

Like the ruling Maravars of Ramnad, the Kallars of Pudukkottai mounted their military power upon an elaborate subcaste organisation which extended the reach of the Kallar Tondaiman raja's authority over the whole of Pudukkottai. The Tondaimans, while still one of several major Kallar chiefly houses, served as fighters under the Sethupati rulers of Ramnad; eventually they entered marriage relations with the Sethupati family, which secured the more reliable military services of the Tondaiman chiefs to the former and also added prestige to the Tondaiman lineage by differentiating them from other Kallar chiefs. That was in the late seventeenth century when lesser Kallar chiefs also subordinated themselves to the Tondaiman chiefs, accepting their protection in return for which these chiefs provided the Kallar Tondaiman rulers with military service. Ruling authority by Tondaimans as well as by lesser Kallar chiefs was shared and was constantly reaffirmed by transactions of durbar deference from Kallar chiefs and royal honours conferred by the Tondaimans.

Like Maravars, the Kallars of Pudukkottai based their warrants for local rule (*patta*) upon protection (*kaval*) of people and their localities, hence upon the right of *pattakaval*. Kallar chiefs, *araiyar*, as protectors (*deskavalkaran*) also patronised temples and Brahmans; and for their protection and king-like patronage, they received a share of agricultural production as well as first temple honours. By the sixteenth century, several Kallar chiefly families began to assume royal titles and prerogatives on the claim of serving the Vijayanagara kings; one of these was the Tondaiman chief.

Tondaiman traditions collected by Colin Mackenzie's ubiquitous Brahmans recorded seventeen generations of rulers between the seventeenth and nineteenth centuries. They were kings within Pudukkottai and also proudly bore the title of poligars as military servants of the nayaka kings of Madurai and as protectors of one of the bastions of the Madurai fort. Along with other Kallar chiefs, the Tondaimans of Pudukkottai served other great households of the southern peninsula, including the Sethupatis of Ramnad and the nayakas of Tanjavur. All of these great lordships recognised the local lordship of the Tondaimans, with the highest honour and recognition being the title 'Raja Tondaiman' conferred by the last of the Vijayanagara kings, Sri Ranga III, who died in 1672.

Kallars were political masters of Pudukkottai, even though they were a majority in only a few parts of the realm. Their authority originated from clan rights they enjoyed in various parts of the territory, which entitled them to hold superior land rights as well as such offices as village or locality headmen. Kallar clans, or subcastes, were called *nadu*, an ancient Tamil term designating a tract of land or an assembly of groups controlling the tract. Each clan territory might consist of some fifteen villages and in the principality as a whole there were thirty of these territories, each with its Kallar chief and its major temple sheltering a local tutelary (usually a goddess) under the protection and patronage of the locality chief.

Rights to land by Kallar clansmen derived from an ancient conquest, but they were fortified by warrants (*patta*) issued by the Kallar Tondaiman raja. Dirks found that about two-thirds of all cultivable land in Pudukkottai was held under such warrants from the raja, a massive degree of royal largesse. As in the heartland of Vijayanagara, temples and Brahmans were the principal holders of these lands (45 per cent) on which no or very low taxes were due; but unlike the Vijayanagara heartland, with its hundred or so major chiefly families, one third of the alienated land in Pudukkottai was held as nearly autonomous domains by several collateral members of the royal lineage who were responsible for maintaining a large portion of the 8,000 or so fighters (*amarakarar*), the core of the raja's forces during the eighteenth century. These Kallar fighters served under commanders drawn mostly from affinal kinsmen holding large landed estates. It seems probable that in earlier times the proportion of cultivable land alienated to support soldiers of the Tondaiman rajas was as high as that granted to the support of temples and Brahmans. It is obvious, therefore, that only a very small revenue could have been raised from the land by the seventeenth-century Tondaiman rajas since the bulk of these revenues were in the hands of Kallar chiefs composing the core of their soldiers.

Lacking the large money incomes of the Tanjavur and Gingee nayakas, where the share claimed by the ruler from the substantial surplus of grain could be contracted to merchants for sale elsewhere in the peninsula, or overseas, most lordships of the southern peninsula during the sixteenth and seventeenth centuries were fiscally dependent upon taxes from commodity production. This would have to be true for the Tondaimans whose territory was an established trade corridor linking the Fishery Coast with the Kaveri and interior Kongu (Coimbatore and Salem) and thence with Arabian Sea ports. The most important sources of commercial revenue consisted of customs collected on goods transiting the realms of the numerous lordships of the time, taxes raised from producers of non-agricultural commodities, especially cotton, indigo, and textiles; taxes on mercantile establishments, bazaars and fairs; and tribute paid by European or Muslim traders who conducted their trade at and usually controlled any ports that might lie in any realm. To tap these sources of state revenue required that rulers of the sixteenth and seventeenth centuries involved the more substantial merchants of their realms or attracted others to act as their money agents and their negotiators with foreign trade-groups and to take tax-farmers.

Pre-eminent among such moneyed men were the 'portfolio capitalists' that Subrahmanyam spoke of; such men were the Malaya family of Telugu merchants, founded by one Achyutappa Chetti at the turn of the seventeenth century. He began serving the Dutch Company on the Gingee coast as a translator and broker around 1608 and was engaged by them to negotiate a trade agreement with the nayaka of Gingee for the creation of a port in his territory at Porto Novo. This successfully completed, Achyutappa became more deeply involved with the Dutch as their principal banker. His Dutch connection did not inhibit an approach to the rival English East India Company with an offer to procure textiles. By the 1630s, Achyutappa and his brother Chinnana had become the major procurement agents for the Dutch in Tanjavur as well as Gingee, and both had also become shipowners and exporters on their own accounts, trading with Sri Lanka, Burma, and Malaya. The brothers also began to farm revenues in the Gingee and Chandragiri territories, especially around the ports of Pulicat, Puducheri, and Porto Novo. In these ways, these traders and other merchants and bankers contributed to the increasing trade along Coromandel and to the generation of new and large taxes for the lords of Gingee, Tanjavur, and Chandragiri. In return, the merchants gained administrative powers as tax collectors to back their diverse commercial and banking enterprises. Seshadra, a nephew of Achyutappa, later became the powerful chief merchant of the English Company at Madras, thereby forging another of the many links between later Vijayanagara institutions and the new era of British dominance that was beginning to take shape in the southern peninsula.

SIX

CONCLUSION

The Tondaiman chief received his title of raja from the last of the Vijayanagara kings, a strange and ironic conferment. For this was a symbolic entitling of a 'little king', already master of a small realm, by the last of a line of kings that had dominated the southern peninsula for three centuries, but who was master of little more than titles to be exchanged for military services he desperately needed merely to stay alive. But more linked the beleaguered Sri Ranga III and the Tondaiman raja than an entitlement, which hardly created the rajadom of Pudukkottai. The more significant connections were of another sort which had to do with what had become essential about the Vijayanagara kingdoms from the fifteenth century on.

The Vijayanagara epoch saw the transition of South Indian society from its medieval past to its modern future. During the time that the rayas were peninsular overlords and their capital the symbol of vast power and wealth, south Indian society was transformed in several important ways. Through most of the first dynasty, Vijayanagara kings were content to be conquerors whose *digivajaya*, or righteous conquests, of Tamil country left the ancient Cholas and Panyas in their sovereign places, except that they were reduced by their homage to Vijayanagara. Until the early sixteenth century, the latter were ritual sovereigns everywhere outside their Deccan heartland; apart from occasional plundering forays, they were content with the homage of distant lords.

Krishnadevaraya changed much of this. He replaced earlier royal predecessors by his own Brahmans and military commanders – the great Telugu nayakas – and charged his agents to extract money tribute from subordinate lords who had previously been required to pay nothing to Vijayanagara, merely to acknowledge the latter's hegemony in a number of symbolic ways, including the acceptance of an important role in temple affairs by royally sponsored sectarian leaders. Economic relations became increasingly monetised as a result of the demands upon rayas and chiefs alike to pay for soldiers, arms, and horses, demands which were made possible by the vast increase in gold and silver from the international demand for Indian commodities. Urban settlements proliferated both to stimulate and then to tap the increasingly generalised exchange of the southern peninsula as well as to serve as fortified headquarters of military lordships – Pudukkottai, the capital of the Tondaimans, meant 'new fort'. Temples of the epoch fed this urbanising process as these institutions became the arenas where the new stratum of local lords – often outsiders – sought to ingratiate their armed rule by raising local deities to new, august statuses. Throughout the Vijayanagara period, but especially after 1500, the pace of agricultural expansion quickened from older zones of riverine cultivation to drier, upland tracts for centuries, bringing whole new regions under the plough and commodities like cotton and indigo into markets to supply a textile industry growing ever larger to meet external demand.

In the beginning, the Vijayanagara kingdom was not very different from its medieval predecessors, Hoysalas and Kakatiyas. But one difference there was, and it explained why the latter two kingdoms were replaceable. That was the urgency to develop better military means to cope with Muslim newcomers to the peninsula. The Sangama founders of Vijayanagana knew the new conditions better than most, having been victims of Muslim expansion against Kakatiya and having later taken service under their Muslim conquerors. The lesson of improved war capability was dearly learned until the fifteenth century when Vijayanagara rulers began incorporating Muslim and later European fighters into their forces. Whatever the lost dharmic credentials of this decision – which seems to have meant more to twentieth-century historians than to the Vijayanagara contemporaries – it was more than compensated by an enhanced ability to hold off Muslim predations and, later, to allow counter-incursions into sultanate territories.

But this very success bore other costs for the kingdom. Paying for mercenaries, their guns, and for better war-horses meant violating ancient institutional immunities protected by previous south Indian lordships and communities. Thus, Krishnadevaraya cast aside the ancient Chola and Pandya kings in the South and installed military commanders who not long after established centres of sovereignty opposed to his successors. Indeed, all kings from Devaraya II in the middle of the fifteenth century to Sriranga III were as often captives of their powerful generalissimos as their masters; and in the Tamil country and Karnataka, at least, the whole of an ancient system of local ruling institutions was attacked by military men whose credentials to rule were gained from their service in Vijayanagara armies.

Still, many earlier communal forms – entitlements and institutions – remained in the late seventeenth century when the last of the Vijayanagara regimes was established in Pudukkottai. Rights and immunities originating from royal grants to Brahmans, temples and even to certain of the cultivating groups of the river valleys continued to be honoured and protected by overlords; and powerful kinship-based authorities – such as the Tondaiman rajas of Pudukkottai – were able to resist attacks upon their clan-based power by dint of their military abilities. Not even the new era of sultans of the eighteenth century – the Mysore usurpers Haidar Ali Khan and Tipu Sultan and the Mughal-sponsored Nawab of Arcot – could extirpate communal rights in their domains. Thus, dual sovereignty continued. On the one hand, there were intrusive royal powers and prebendal entitlements, and, on the other hand, there remained communally derived and sustained entitlements. The latter were destined to be strongly entrenched when the British assumed their territorial rule in the late eighteenth century.

These two sources of authority can be variously designated, as royal and chiefly, central and local, prebendal and communal; they were not introduced during the Vijayanagara period, but much earlier. In Chola times royal gifts to individual or groups of Brahmans as *brahmadeya* may be understood as the joint action of a king or his agent and the major landholding and sometimes commercial groups of a locality (i.e., *nadu*) acting corporately as the people of the locality, or *nattar*. Enormous Brahman villages were created in Tamil country by such joint enactments, which often included immunities from local demands and protection by local chiefs as well as distant kings. However, enactments such as these were restricted to Brahmans or temples then. Similar collective entitlements continued to be awarded in Vijayanagara times, though seldom for the great Brahman villages of old. During Vijayanagara times, temples became the major recipients of royal and chiefly largesse, and, as in earlier days, this involved undertakings between royals, or their agents, and temple managers who were appointed and supported by local chieftains. But in Vijayana-gara times, wholly new prebendal entitlements came into being of which *amara*, or *nayankara*, entitlements were the most general and penetrating.

It was, after all, military modernisation that spurred the trans-formation of the late medieval South Indian state – improved war-horses and archers to match those of the Muslim fighters and guns which they also introduced. Monetisation and urbanisation, while shaped by religious and commercial processes, as well as political, also supported the military programme of Vijayanagara rulers, beginning in the fifteenth century. Europeans, when they appeared, intensified the commercial and monetising forces har-nessed by Vijayanagara kings of the sixteenth century, and Portu-guese soldiers added necessary gunnery skills to the armies of Krishnadevaraya and his successors.

None of these developments required or generated a substantially more centralised administration in the kingdom. Administrative forms of the fifteenth and sixteenth centuries certainly improved and were widely adopted by all lordships. But the model for this improved administration was more the temples of the age than the Vijayanagara state apparatus, which remained primitive. Krishnade-varaya's considered appointment of Brahmans to higher offices, including military ones such as fortress commanders, was reversed by Aliya Rama Raja within twenty years, and a more pervasively patri-monial regime was created involving as its principal actors the great Telugu households of the sixteenth century. It was the unleashing of armed competition among these Telugu houses that prevented the restoration of vigorous royal authority after the defeat of 1565.

Different configuring factors operated in the contemporary Deccani sultanates. As already noted, the Muslim rulers of Gol-konda made large accommodations to the sub-stratum of Telugu territorial chiefs of their realm. They and the sultans of Bijapur offered military service to and patronage for the cultural and religious institutions of their Hindu subjects; both also left terri-torial chiefs in undiminished, if not enhanced, authority in their local domains. In this, neither regime had much choice, since each was based upon an élite of Muslim warriors that was Deccani, not foreign, in culture and affinity and whose numbers were never so

great as to overwhelm local, ancient, Hindu lordships. Notwithstanding these limitations upon the ambitions of these Muslim
regimes, theirs were more powerfully centralised polities than
Vijayanagara. Though they were rooted in their Deccan situation by
generations of coresidence and even inter-marriage with Hindus,
the ruling warrior and learned élite of these sultanates were self-
consciously Muslim, and that Islamic identity and its institutions
(such as the robust Sufi tradition of Bijapur analysed by R. M.
Eaton) provided an ideological frame very different from that of
Vijayanagara. No notion of shared sovereignty, claims of *dayada*,
were brooked in Golkonda or Bijapur, however substantial the
degree of local power held by Reddi, Velama or Maratha chiefs,
whereas this was the core of Vijayanagara sovereignty from first to
last. Also, prebendal rights conferred by Muslim regimes, whether
to Muslim grandees or to such devoted servants of Bijapur as Shahji
Bhonsle, were less easily transformed into hereditary chiefly rights,
though – as Frank Perlin has shown – such communal appropriations did occur among some of the great service and chiefly
households of Maharashtra during the seventeenth century. One
other factor lent a relatively greater potential for central power to
the Golkonda regime, at least. This was their direct involvement in
the rich Coromandel trade as active administrators and as traders,
both of which brought resources for strengthening their central
authority beyond any available to the Vijayanagara kings.

Nevertheless, everywhere in the southern peninsula, among the
warring Telugu imperial houses, the more prudent nayaka kingdoms, and the great host of lesser lords, prebendal rights began to
compete with as well as to complement older communal ones. The
eventual stand-off between these two fundamentally different forms
of right can be attributed to the persistent strength of the latter and
to the fact that prebendal rights from the start in Vijayanagara – as
elsewhere in India and elsewhere in the pre-modern world – always
tended to become hereditary and hence were lost to royal, central,
or service-connected employment. Thus, the effect in many parts of
the Vijayanagara South was merely to introduce a new stratum of
power and authority. Most conspicuously, this consisted of Telugu
and Kannadiga military agents of the rayas in Tamil country, but it
also included the enhancing of the authority of some local chiefs

against others (such as the Tondaiman Kallar against other Kallars) and some local groups against others (such as the Vanniyar peasant-warriors against Arcot Vellalars).

The Vijayanagara transformation of the old regime out of which its early rulers emerged was not complete by the late seventeenth century, but it was an irreversible change from that old order. In fact, the supersession of local chiefs as the protectors of the structure of communal rights by centralised authority in the peninsula was not accomplished until British times. Neither the Marathas nor the Muslim sultans of Mysore – Haidar Ali and Tipu Sultan – achieved this end, though that is precisely what the latter strenuously sought.

This is a major reason for continuing to think of the Vijayanagara kingdom as a segmentary state. In such a polity, historical community entitlements and institutions remain vigorous. It is true that communal rights and such rights protecting bodies as the *nadu* in Tamil country were weakened by the imposition of Vijayanagara prebendal rights. But the latter in their turn strengthened other local institutions, such as local chiefs and temples. This was both a symptom and a consequence of the weak prebendalism of Vijayanagara which, in its turn, manifested the weakly centralised character of that kingdom. Its élite stratum of warrior chiefs easily and continuously transformed rights gained from the state, with their attendant authority and military powers into more formidable chieftaincies. In the long run, and despite Krishnadevaraya's efforts, this defeated any attempt to increase centralised authority in the kingdom. Only by fundamentally changing the balance between its kings and its ruling chiefs as was more successfully accomplished in the Muslim conquest states of the Deccan could that balance have been shifted. Both local chiefly authority and ancient, though modified, community rights remained intact structures in the southern peninsula until the early nineteenth-century consolidation of colonial power there. This was the impressive legacy of the segmentary politics and society of the Vijayanagara age.

Thomas Munro, a shaper of the colonial regime in the peninsula grasped this point firmly while he was a young soldier in the East India Company army. He seemed to see that Haidar Ali Khan and his son, Tipu Sultan, had the ability and the determination to achieve the elusive quest for an effectively-centralised political system. This

would have been along the lines of Krishnadevaraya, by subordinating chiefly authority. In 1790, he wrote to his father in Scotland
comparing the Maratha and Mysore regimes and criticising his
superiors who thought the Marathas the greater threat to English
supremacy in the peninsula. Tipu Sultan's regime, Munro wrote,

> is the most simple and despotic monarchy in the world, in which
> every department, civil and military, possesses the regularity and
> system communciated to it by the genius of Hyder, and in which
> all pretensions derived from high birth being discouraged, all
> independent chiefs ... subjected or extirpated, justice severely and
> impartially administered ... a numerous and well-disciplined
> army kept up, and almost every employment of trust and con-
> sequence conferred on men raised from obscurity gives the
> government a vigour hitherto unexampled in India. [Marathas, by
> contrast, were] ... a confederation of independent chiefs possess-
> ing extensive dominions, and numerous armies, now acting in
> concert, now jealous of each other, and acting for their own
> advantage, and at all times liable to be detached from the public
> cause ... can never be a dangerous enemy to the English.[1]

Krishnaswami Aiyangar, in the earliest phase of Vijayanagara
historiography proposed that the flame of Vijayanagara passed
directly to the Marathas and meant by this the defence of Hindu
society and culture, which he and other Indian nationalist historians
considered the mission of the Vijayanagara kingdom. That ideological framing of Vijayanagara history is rejected here. However,
the structure of politics in both the Vijayanagara and Maratha
kingdoms was certainly similar, as Munto implicitly observed. This
similarity derived from the same general processes that fundamentally altered the political economy of the Deccan inherited from
the ancient Chalukyan kingdom at Badami and set both Vijayanagara and Maratha kingdoms upon a road to more centralised and
effective rule, which neither, however, fully travelled.

[1] G. R. Gleig, *The Life of Major-General Sir Thomas Munro, Bart. and K.C.B., Late Governor of Madras*, London, 1830, vol. 1, pp. 84–5.

BIBLIOGRAPHICAL ESSAY

I SOURCES

Full translations and summaries of inscriptions from the Tamil, Telugu, and Kannada continue to be published by the Archaeological Survey of India in *South Indian Inscriptions* and *Epigraphia Indica*, as well as in inscriptional series of Tamilnadu State, Andhra Pradesh and Karnataka; Lewis Rice's multi-volumed *Epigraphia Carnatica* of the Mysore Archaeological Series (16 volumes, 1889–1955) has now been substantially revised and extended and may be republished in the near future. Glossaries such as D. C. Sircar's *Indian Epigraphical Glossary*, Delhi, 1966, indexes such as *Annual Report on South Indian Epigraphy*, which date from 1887 and summarise newly copied inscriptions, and other reference aids for using inscriptions provide access to this primary source, permitting the reader to go beyond the readings which follow.

Literary sources from the Vijayanagara period, ranging from complete translations to abbreviated summaries, have long been available, beginning with S. Krishnaswami Aiyangar's *The Sources of Vijayanagara History*, Madras, 1919, and continuing with the much larger *Further Sources of Vijayanagara History*, 3 vols; edited by K. A. Nilakanta Sastri and N. Venkataramanayya, Madras, 1946. To these were added the valuable translations of the oral and manuscript accounts collected by Colin Mackenzie during the early nineteenth century under the editorial direction of T. V. Mahalingam, *Mackenzie Manuscripts; Summaries of the Historical Manuscripts in the Mackenzie Collection*, 2 vols., Madras, 1972.

2 GENERAL WRITING

Two types of general works on the Vijayanagara kingdom may be distinguished: one that attempts to cover all major aspects of the history of the kingdom and another that treats some specific aspects over the entire history. Pride of place among histories of the kingdom has usually gone to Robert Sewell's *A Forgotten Empire (Vijayanagar)*, London, 1900; however, this work is valuable not so much for its treatment of the whole of the history of the kingdom as for its translations of Portuguese sources of the sixteenth century. Sewell's contributions to the opening of Vijayanagara history are better represented in other of his works upon which other early historians substantially drew and through which the first generation of Indian historians of the kingdom became familiar with modern, European historical methods. Among these other works of Sewell are: 'List of the Inscriptions and Sketch of the Dynasties of Southern India' and 'List of the Antiquarian Remains in the Presidency of Madras', published in *Archaeological Survey of Southern India*, vols. 1 and 2, Madras, 1882; *The Historical Inscriptions of Southern India (collected till 1923) and Outlines of Political History*, edited and completed by S. Krishnaswami Aiyangar (Madras, 1932). The latter went on to make the most important contributions to the general history of Vijayanagara in his *Ancient India*, Madras, 1911; *South India and Her Muhammadan Invaders*, Madras, 1921; and his *Evolution of Hindu Administrative Institutions of Southern India*, Madras, 1931. By then, the 1930s, there was a flowering of Vijayanagara studies that included the publication of *Further Sources* for which N. Venkataramanayya prepared a monograph-length general historical introduction. In addition, Karnatak historians produced a large volume commemorating the founding of the kingdom three hundred years before – *Vijayanagara Sexcentenary Commemoration Volume*, Dharwar, 1936, containing studies of religion, art history, architecture, and literature as well as conventional political history. A major point of the volume and a good part of its argumentation was to oppose a 'Telugu' interpretation of the founding of kingdom in 1336 that had been presented in several works of N. Venkataramanayya, beginning with his 1929 monograph, *Kampili and Vijayanagara*, Madras, and reinforced by his monumental, *Studies in the Third Dynasty of Vijayanagara*, Madras, 1935. Another publication of about the same time was B. A. Saletore's University of London doctoral thesis of 1931 under the title *Social and Political Life in the Vijayanagara Empire*, 2 vols., Madras, 1934. Several synthetic histories of the Vijayanagara kingdom were produced in the next two decades culminating in K. A. Nilakanta Sastri's two long chapters in his *A History of South India*, Madras, 1955.

Other works that treat some aspect of the whole of Vijayanagara history include studies of other regional polities of the Vijayanagara period: A. Krishnaswami Pillai, *The Tamil Country under Vijayanagara*, Annamalai, 1964; K. A. Nilakanta Sastri, *The Pandyan Kingdom from the Earliest Times to the Sixteenth Century*, London, 1929; K. V. Ramesh, *A History of South Kanara*, Dharwar, 1970; M. D. Sampath, *Chittoor Through the Ages*, Delhi, 1980; H. K. Sherwani and P. M. Joshi, *History of Medieval Deccan (1295–1724)*, 2 vols., Hyderabad, 1973; P. Gururaja Bhatt, *Studies in Tuluva History and Culture*, Manipal, 1975; G. Yazdani, *The Early History of the Deccan*, 2 vols., Oxford, 1960; H. Krishna Sastri, 'The First [Second and Third] Vijayanagara Dynasty: Its Viceroys and Ministers', *Archaeological Survey of India; Annual Report, 1907–8, 1908–9, 1911–12*, Calcutta, 1911–13; 'The Ajnapatra or Royal Edict'. *The Journal of Indian History* 8, 1929, 83–105; 207–33; V. D. Rao, 'Ajnyapatra Re-examined', *The Journal of Indian History* 29, 1951, 63–89. In addition, there were studies of social and economic aspects of Vijayanagara society found in: A. Appadorai, *Economic Conditions in Southern India (A.D.*

1000–1500) 2 vols., Madras, 1936; T. V. Mahalingam, *Administration and Social Life under Vijayanagara*, Madras, 1940; and his *Economic Life in the Vijayanagara Empire*, Madras, 1951; Vijaya Ramaswamy, 'Artisans in Vijayanagar Society', *Indian Economic and Social History Review* 22, 1985, 417–44; B. Stein, *Peasant State and Society in Medieval South India*, Delhi, 1980, and B. Stein (ed.), *South Indian Temples; An Analytical Reconstruction*, New Delhi, 1978; B. A. Saletore, *Medieval Jainism with Special Reference to the Vijayanagara Empire*, Bombay, 1938; T. K. T. Viraraghavacharya, *History of Tirupati*, 2 vols., Tirupati, Andhra Pradesh, 1953. Other valuable studies include: F. C. Danvers, *The Portuguese in India*, 2 vols., London, 1894; Tapan Raychudhuri, *Jan Company in Coromandel*, 'S-Gravenhage, 1962; T. Raychaudhuri and I. Habib, *The Cambridge Economic History of India*, vol. 1, Cambridge, 1982; and D. Ludden, *Peasant History in South India*, Princeton, 1985.

3 PREDECESSORS, FOUNDERS AND LOSERS

The conditions under which the kingdom was established in the fourteenth century are analysed in the following works: J. D. M Derrett, *The Hoysalas. A Medieval Indian Royal Family*, London, 1957; H. K. Sherwani, *The Bahmanis of the Deccan*, Hyderabad, 1953; M. Somasekhara Sarma, *History of the Reddi Kingdom (ca. A.D. 1325 to ca. A.D. 1488)*, Waltair, Andhra Pradesh, 1948; Vasundhara Filliozat, *L'Epigraphie de Vijayanagara du début à 1377*, Paris, 1973, and her *La Rāmāyana à Vijayanagar*, Paris, 1983; M. Habib (ed.), *A Comprehensive History of India*, vol. 5, *The Delhi Sultanate (A.D. 1206–1526)*, Delhi, 1970. A valuable discussion of the historical debate about the origins of the first dynasty of the kingdom and whether they were from Karnataka or Andhra is found in Hermann Kulke, 'Maharajas, Mahants and Historians. Reflections on the Historiography of Early Vijayanagara and Sringiri', in A. L. Dallapiccola (ed.), *Vijayanagara – City and Empire*, vol. 1, Stuttgart, 1985, 120–44.

4 VIJAYANAGARA: THE CITY

The earliest of the long list of descriptions of the city are contemporary, beginning with Nicolo de Conti's of about 1420, contained in R. H. Major (ed.), *India in the Fifteenth Century. Being a Collection of Narratives of voyages to India* ... London, 1857, and a later set of descriptions commenced with the colonial report on the city of E.C Ravenshaw, 'Translation of Various Inscriptions found among the Ruins of Vijayanagar ...' *Asiatic Researches* 20, 1836. More contemporary descriptions are had from A. H. Longhurst, *Hampi Ruins, Described and Illustrated*, Calcutta, 1917 and G. Michell and V. Filliozat, *Splendours of the Vijayanagara Empire: Hampi*, Bombay, *Marg*, 1981; M. S. Nagaraja Rao, *Vijayanagara – Progress of Research, 1979–83 [1983–84]*, Mysore, 1983 and 1985; J. Fritz,

G. Michell, and M. S. Nagaraja Rao, *The Royal Centre at Vijayanagara, Preliminary Report*, Melbourne, 1984. The most recent and comprehensive scholarly discussions of the capital city in its imperial setting can be found in the set of essays edited by A. Dallapiccola, *Vijayanagara – City and Empire*, 2 vols., Stuttgart, 1985.

5 TRIUMPH AND DÉBÂCLE

Venkataramanayya's *Studies in the Third Dynasty*, of over half a century ago, continues to be the authoritative interpretation of the early sixteenth-century kingdom; Henry Heras, *The Aravidu Dynasty of Vijayanagara*, Madras, 1927, continues the political account to the end of the kingdom in the seventeenth century. A valuable recent work on the contemporary economy is S. Subrahmanyam, 'Trade and the Regional Economy of South India, *c.* 1550 to 1650', unpublished doctoral thesis, Department of Economics, Delhi School of Economics, 1986, and forthcoming from Cambridge. While there are several translation projects of the Telugu poem, 'Amukatamalyada' attributed to King Krishnadevaraya, reliance must still be placed on the partial translation of A. Rangasvami Sarasvati, 'Political Maxims of the Emperor-Poet, Krishnadeva Raya', *The Journal of Indian History* 4, 1925, 61–88; there is a biographical study of this king by M. Rama Rao, *Krishnadevaraya*, New Delhi, 1971. Sewell's older translation of the Portuguese Paes and Nuniz has been re-examined in, *The Vijayanagara Empire: As Seen by Domingo Paes and Fernão Nuniz, Two Sixteenth-Century Chroniclers*, edited by V. Filliozat, New Delhi, 1977; and the following works are important on Tamil localised societies of the time: N. Karashima, *South Indian History and Society; Studies from Inscriptions, A.D. 850–1800*, Delhi, 1984; Y. Subbarayalu, 'The Peasantry of the Tiruchirappalli District from the Thirteenth to the Seventeenth Centuries', *Studies in Socio-Cultural Change in Rural Villages in Tiruchirappalli District, Tamilnadu, India*, Tokyo, 1980; N. Karashima, 'Nayaka Rule in North and South Arcot Districts in South India during the Sixteenth Century', *Acta Asiatica [Tokyo]*, 48, 1985.

6 SIMULTANEOUS AND SUCCESSOR REGIMES

The defeat of Vijayanagara and the sack of the city in 1565 by the confederacy of sultanate forces ushered in a period of extended chaos and decline that is treated both generally and in terms of Tamil country by R. Sathianathaier, *Tamilaham in the Seventeenth Century*, Madras, 1956; other important studies of the era are: the same author's (under the name R. Sathyanatha Aiyar) *History of the Nayaks of Madura*, Madras, 1924; K. D. Swaminathan, *The Nayakas of Ikkeri*, Madras, 1957; V. Vriddhagirisan, *The Nayaks of Tanjore*, Annamalainagar, 1942; C. Hayavadana Rao, *History of Mysore*, 2 vols., Bangalore, 1948. This later period has been analysed in historical–cultural terms by N. B. Dirks, *The Hollow Crown; Ethnohistory of an Indian Kingdom*, Cambridge, 1988 and B. E. F. Beck, *Peasant Society in Konku*, Vancouver, 1972, while aspects of political developments, especially in Andhra, are found in J. F. Richards, *Mughal Administration in Golconda*, Oxford, 1975.

7 THINGS TO COME

The current efflorescence of Vijayanagara studies has made the present work different in many ways from previous works, but, because some of the best of the most recent work consists of unpublished theses available principally in India, and there on a restricted basis, citation of them is pointless for the general reader. However, these studies will be published in the coming years and therefore mention should be made of them here. Among the most valuable of such studies are theses of the Centre for Historical Studies, Jawaharlal Nehru University including those of J. Lakshmi, on Telengana; Ravi Palat on northern Tamil country; and C. N. Subramanian on Tanjavur. Other similar research that has proven useful is the Aligarh Muslim University thesis of Parvathi Menon on the Carnatic; the University of Hawaii thesis of Venkata Raghotham on Tamil country; and the University of Wisconsin thesis of Philip Wagoner on the 'Rayavacakamu'. The Vijayanagara project of the Karnataka State Department of Archaeology, whose publications are cited above, continues to produce archaeological and art-historical documentation from Hampi, and new work is in progress on translations and analysis of Vijayanagara period texts in Tamil and Telugu, involving Velcheru Narayana Rao, David Shulman, Sanjay Subrahmanyam and others. All of this buttresses the tens of thousands of published stone and copper-plate inscriptional records that have constituted the foundation of Vijayanagara history.

INDEX

Abdar Razzaq, 36
Achyutadevaraya, 58, 82; communal
  entitlements, 108; Deccan sultanates,
  116; rebellions, 57, 68–9, 89–90, 99,
  116, 124; temples, 38, 89
administration, 87, 90; Brahmans, 93–4,
  124; modes, 86; temples, 88–90, 96;
  village and locality, 86
agricultural frontier, 21, 44, 96, 105, 141,
Ahmadnagar sultan Burhan Khan
  (1509–53), 117
Ahobalam, 102, 112; mathas, 103
Ain-i-Akbari, 65, 75
Ajnapatra of Banahatti, 24, 94–5, 105
Ala-ud-Din Khalji, 22
Aliya Rama Raja 48, 50, 58, 68, 80, 83–4,
  88–90, 112, 121; and Achyutadevaraya,
  67; and Portuguese, 118; biographical,
  113; brothers Tirumala and Venkatadri,
  118; commanders, 92; customs wealth,
  119; Muslim soldiers, 69; nephew Vithala,
  114–15; patrimonial politics, 124, 143;
  rebellions, 93; supporters in Rayalaseema,
  118
Aluvakonda, 86–9, 93, 130
amaram grant for military service, 86,
  143
Anantapur Hande chiefs, 88
Anegondi, 18–19, 34; chiefs, 59
Appadurai, Arjun, 65–6, 76
Aravidi Bukka, 55, 71, 113; son Tirumala,
  120
Aravidu lineage, 1, 122
Ariyanatha Mudaliar, 57
Asad Khan of Belgaum, 116
Ashokan edicts, 31
ayagar system, 7

Badami, 18
Bahmani sultanate, 19, 27–8, 30, 46, 67;
  Muhammed I and Mujahid (c. 1358–78),
  115
Bangaluru or Bangalore, 82–3
Bankapur, 58
Bedars or Boyas, 60
Bhatkal, 127
Bijapur sultanate, 43, 68, 113, 122, 127;
  Ibrahim Adil Shahi, 114, 117; invasions,
  123

brahmadeya or *agrahara* (Brahman
  settlements), 79, 84, 142
Brahmans, 88; accountants and scribes, 86;
  administrators, 81; landed communities,
  79
Bukka I (1344–77), 19, 27–8, 92
Bullock transport, 101

cash crops, 24
cash revenue demands, 41
caste, 102
Chalukyas of Badami, 1, 13, 54, 111, 146
Chalukyas of Kalyani, 16–17
Chaudhuri, K. N., 25
chiefs, 43, 70, 73, 87, 105, 144; and
  temples, 103, 145; coalitions, 109, 117,
  125; Lingayat, 60; marriage ties, 124;
  protectors of communal rights, 110, 145;
  scattered interests, 87
Chinese porcelain, 35
Chitradurga or Chitaldrug, 85
Chola kingdom, 7–8, 14, 16–17, 20, 42,
  54–5, 57, 61–2, 141; capitals, 35; history,
  9–10; resource base, 15; royal gifts, 142;
  temples, 32, 111
civil war 1542–3, 114, 121–3
coastal trade, 127
Cochin, 127
commercialisation, 76–7, 101, 110; and
  chiefs, 85; temples, 101
commodity production, 53–4, 141; cotton
  and indigo, 101
communal, 96; agrarian rights, 104; control
  of irrigation, 100; ('community') defined,
  101–2; élites, 98–101; entitlements and
  institutions, 63–4, 70, 95–6, 106, 142,
  144; property, 96, 130; resistance, 97

dayada or shared sovereignty, 24, 63, 105; in
  Golkonda and Bijapur, 144
Deccan sultanates, 75, 93, 115; and
  Krishnadevaraya, 116; compared
  Vijayanagara, 143–4; grand alliance of
  1564, 117, 119, 120
Derrett, J. D. M., 45
Devagiri (renamed Daulatabad), 22
Devaraya I (1406–24), 28–9; communal
  entitlements, 108
Devaraya II (1424–46), 29–30, 38, 42, 71–2;

INDEX

Mirasidar, 98
monetisation, 47, 65, 73–4, 143
money taxes, 41, 64
Mughals 122
Muhammad bin Tughlak, 18, 19, 23
Muhammad Kasim Firishtah, 5
Munro, Thomas, 58–9, 129, 145
Muslims: cavalry, 22; chiefs, 60; chronicles, 5, 8; conquest, 20; converts, 23; soldiers in Vijayanagara, 29, 109, 120; trade, 74–5; warriors Deccani culture, 143
Mysore kingdom, 69, 146; chiefs 134–5; Chamaraja (1513–53), 82; foundation, 132; Raja Wodeyar (1578–1617), 82

Nagama Nayaka, 57
Narasa Nayaka, 29, 71
Nattar leaders of the nadu, 63, 78, 142
Nawab of Arcot, 142
Nayaka kingdoms, 63; commerce and commodity production, 131; origins 121; ritual aspects, 133; 'successor states', 69, 121, 131–2 taxes from commodity production, 138; temples, 112; territoriality, 130
Nayaka kingdom of Gingee, 123, 134
Nayaka kingdom of Ikkeri, 69, 84, 132; chiefs, 134–5; Sadasiva Nayaka (1540–65), 84, 117–18; Venkatappa Nayaka (1586–1629), 123, 130
Nayaka kingdom of Madurai, 80, 114, 123; invasion of Mysore, 135; Krishnappa, 57, 119; military dependencies, 133; Tirumala Nayaka (1623–59), 130; Tirunelveli, 114; Visvanatha, 114
Nayaka kingdom of Tanjavur, 98, 122; and landed élite, 134; Sivappa Nayaka, 57
Nayankara system, 7, 143
Nilakanta Sastri, K. A., 7–11, 110
Nuniz, Fernão, 35, 39

Odeyar chiefs, 82

Paes, Domingo, 33–5, 39
Pallava kingdom, 14
Pandya kingdom, 14, 16–17, 42, 55, 57, 61–2, 141; capitals, 35; resource base, 15; temples, 32
patrimonial politics, 92, 125–6, 131; and trade, 125
peasant resistance, 21, 41
Penukonda, 111, 119
Perlin, F., 144
'poligars' (or: palaiyakkarar, palegadu,

palagararu), 43, 59–61, 79, 84, 126, 133, 137; 'Palaiyam' military encampment, 133
politicised temple administration, 96
population, 44–6, 79, 82
Portuguese, 3, 114; chronicles, 5, 8; piracy, 75; soldiers in Vijayanagara, 143; trade rights, 58; Vijayanagara politics, 125
pre-Vijayanagara regimes, 24, 61–3, 70, 72, 141
prebendalism, 64, 81; entitlements, 63, 65, 142, 144
private landed proprietorship, 95
production zones in the peninsula, 128–9
Pulicat, 81, 126–7

Raichur, 18–19, 28, 34, 67, 81, 115–16, 126–7
rajya or province, 28, 42
Ramachandra temple, 32, 33, 35, 37
Ramesh, K. V., 52
Ramesvaram temple, 135
Rayalaseema country, 86, 88; chiefs, 99, 113
Rayavachakamu, 94, 95, 106, 132
Reddi caste, 21, 61, 80; chiefs, 54, 144
Reddi kings of Kondavidu, 28–9
Richards, John, 80
right and left castes, 107–8
Roghair, Gene H., 103

Salakaraju chiefs, 50, 51, 68, 113, 124; Salakaraju Tirumalayadeva, 116
Saletore, B. A., 6–7
Saluva Narasimha (d. 1491), 1, 29, 42, 50–1, 55, 59, 66, 78, 89, 92; chiefs, 93; political changes, 71; preceptor, 102
Saluva Nayaka (Chellappa), 48, 57, 99; rebellion, 50–1, 99
Saluva Timma (minister), 48
Saluva Timmarasu, 49
Sambuvaraya chief of Tondaimandalam, 42, 54–5
Sangama dynasty, 1, 27, 42, 92; and chiefs, 93; sons of Sangama, 19
segmentary polity, 10, 24, 41–2, 62, 91, 92, 145
Sewell, Robert, 2–4, 9, 39
Shahji Bhonsle, 60
Shanar chiefs, 79
Sringiri matha, 84
Srirangapattanam, 59
Srisailam temples and matha, 103, 111
Stein, B., 10
Subbarayalu, Y., 40, 76, 95–6
Subrahmanyam, S., 74, 126–8, 139
Sufi tradition, 144

Tadpatri, 112
Tamil country, 50, 55, 69, 76, 110; chiefs, 45; 'peasant revolt', 77; right and left castes, 77; Saivism, 104

Tanjavur, 57–8, 69
tank irrigation, 21, 24
tax farming, 41, 47, 128–9, 134, 139; Brahmans, 81; Golkonda, 128
Telangana, 45, 54; chiefs, 80; Saivism, 104
Telugus: Balija Chetti merchants, 87, 128, 139; chiefs, 46, 81; cultivators, 45; migrations, 46
temples, 88; accounts, 90; administration, 143; aggregative, 102; and community, 103–5, and politics, 65; commerce, 76; Decan style, 111; irrigation investments, 24, 89–90; urbanisation, 24, 26, 106
Tipu Sultan, 142
Tiruchirappalli, 29; revolt of 1429, 100
Tirunelveli, 15, 78–9
Tirupati–Tirumalai temple complex, 59, 66, 69, 88–9, 102; mathas, 103
Tiruvannamali, 19, 27
trade customs, 42
trans-peninsular trade routes, 39
Travancore, 18, 51; raja Unni Varma, 114
tributary payments, 39, 47
Tughlak sultans, 14
Tuluva dynasty, 27, 29, 31–2, 42–3, 58, 68, 68, 87, 113; and chiefs, 93
Tuticorin, 114

Udayagiri, 28
Ummattur chiefs of Sivasamudram, 43, 50, 56, 83, 93
urbanisation, 24, 107–8, 110, 141, 143; lower orders, 106–7
utaimai or ksattra, 62

Vanniyar peasant-warriors, 21, 99, 145

Velamas, 21, 30, 80; chiefs of Telangana, 28–9, 54, 103, 144; Vaishnavism, 103
Vellalars, 79, 145
Velugoti chiefs, 116; Yachama Nayudu, 122–3
Venkataramanayya N., 6–10, 19, 27, 65
Vijayanagara: a 'segmentary state', 145; assassinations, 91–2, 109; centralising, 94–5, 105; competition of royal lineages, 91–3; coronations, 132–3; foreign policy, 112; ideology, 146; inscriptions, 31; late capitals, 119, 125; mercantilist activities, 129; military modernisation, 29, 43, 95, 119, 141, 143; revenue base, 60–1, 129–30; ruling lineages, 1, 13, 120; Sadasivaraya (1542–76), 69, 114, 120; socio/political transformation, 106, 140–5; studies, 31; Telugu and Kannadiga military agents, 144; temple style, 32, 111–12; use of artillery, 119; usurpations, 27, 91–2, 109; Vira Narasimharaya (1505–9), 87; weak prebendalism, 145
Vijayanagara city, 38, 39; architectural style, 37; as a market, 75; civil monuments, 35, 36; goddess Hampadevi (or Pampadevi), 31; mahanavami festival, 36, 37, 39, 132; Muslim residents, 34; Muslim structures, 35; names, 19, 31; palaces, 35–7, 40; sack of 1565, 80, 81; temple complexes, 32, 34; Virupaksha temple, 112; Vithala temple, 31, 38, 112; zones, 31, 34
village accountants karanam, 86
village and locality headmen, 90, 97, 137
Virasaivas, 103; mathas or seminaries, 85; shrines, 84

war commodities, 22, 74
Warangal, 16, 19
Wilks, Mark, 2, 5

Yadavaraya chiefs of Chandragiri, 42, 54–5

THE NEW CAMBRIDGE HISTORY OF INDIA

I The Mughals and their Contemporaries

II Indian States and the Transition to Colonialism

III The Indian Empire and the Beginnings of Modern Society

IV The Evolution of Contemporary South Asia

* already published

Printed in the United States
79902LV00004B/121-129